God's Representatives

By the same author

Ritualism and Politics in Victorian Britain
Martin Niemöller
Secrets of Mount Sinai
Oberammergau and the Passion Play
Albert Schweizer: The Enigma
Restless Bones: The Story of Relics
The Way of Saint James

GOD'S REPRESENTATIVES

The Eight Twentieth-Century Popes

James Bentley

Constable · London

First published in Great Britain 1997
by Constable and Company Ltd
3 The Lanchesters, 162 Fulham Palace Road
London W6 9ER

ISBN 0 09 476730 0

Set in Linotron Ehrhardt 11pt by
SetSystems Ltd, Saffron Walden
Printed in Great Britain by
St Edmundsbury Press Ltd
Bury St Edmunds, Suffolk

A CIP catalogue record for this book
is available from the British Library

for audrey,

and with thanks to the Franciscans and staff

of the Catholic Central Library in London

Contents

Preface

In our own century, through times of war and times of peace, the papacy has played a delicate, sometimes critical and often controversial role on the world's stage. Popes have occupied themselves not only with questions of faith and morals, but also with politics. While attempting to find a proper response to the twentieth-century dictators (Stalin, Franco, Hitler, Pavelic and Mussolini), they have also pronounced on such contentious moral and practical issues as abortion and contraception, and in religious matters on the inerrancy of the Bible or whether the Blessed Virgin Mary ascended incorrupt into heaven.

As spiritual leaders of the western world, their role has involved them in a century that has seen two world wars and the attempted destruction of the entire Jewish people, as well as a conflict between communism and capitalism that threatened to annihilate many inhabitants of our planet. And since the Catholic Church is today at its strongest outside the boundaries of European Christianity, popes in this century have also inevitably been concerned with the third world and the response of the rich nations to the dispossessed.

This book examines, sometimes critically, sometimes approvingly, the secular and religious work of all eight twentieth-century popes. The first of these is Pius X, who reigned from 1903 to 1914. Declared a saint in 1954, Pius was a man of deep humility and goodness, and equally an uncompromising pontiff. Almost as soon as he was enthroned as pope, he boldly broke off official relations with an increasingly secular France, thereby almost completely impoverishing the French Catholic Church. He refused to receive President Theodore Roosevelt because the president had addressed Methodists in Rome. As for theological concerns, Pius X stringently banned the Modernists: men and women who were attempting to come to terms with twentieth-century thought while remaining Catholics.

His successor, Benedict XV, acceded to the papal throne just as the First World War broke out and reigned till 1922. Benedict XV set himself the impossible task of promoting peace while remaining neutral. As a result, both sides in the conflict distrusted him. In 1917 his seven-point plan proposing an end to the war on grounds of justice rather than military might was massively scorned. Yet after the war he became a strong and popular supporter of the League of Nations. And he succeeded in reconciling to the Vatican not only the French who had been estranged by his predecessor but also the surviving Modernists, as well as many Eastern Orthodox Christians.

The greatest achievement of Pius XI, who succeeded Benedict XV in 1922, was the Lateran Treaty of 1929, negotiated with Mussolini, which was widely criticised. 'Mussolini is a wonderful man,' Pius XI declared. Whatever the truth of this judgement (and the pope lived to regret it), the treaty has remained the bulwark of the Vatican's independence as a neutral state. Pius

XI also supported the régime of General Francisco Franco in Spain. And under his papacy the first treaty between Hitler's Germany and any foreign power was agreed. Yet in 1937, after the Nazis had repeatedly breached this treaty, he published an encyclical branding National Socialism as fundamentally unChristian, a letter read from every German Catholic pulpit on 14 March of that year.

When he died in 1939 he was succeeded by a man who had been his ambassador to Germany. Many have since concluded that Pope Pius XII's admiration for the Germans fatally compromised his attitude to the Third Reich. He never, for instance, publicly protested against the massacre of the Jews; yet some have argued that to have done so would have been useless and have also pointed out that the Vatican did manage to save many Jews from death.

No traditionalist in theological matters, this pope allowed scholars to use modern historical methods to explore the Christian scriptures. At the same time he remained devoted to the cult of the Blessed Virgin Mary, declaring in 1950 that she was bodily assumed into heaven. And he remained implacably opposed to contraception and artificial insemination.

John XXIII, elected in 1958 at the age of seventy-seven as a stop-gap pope, proved to be a revolutionary. He called a major Vatican Council of bishops with the specific objects of bringing the Church up-to-date and setting in motion ways of reuniting western and eastern Christendom. Observers from eighteen non-Roman Catholic Churches were given seats of honour at the council. His reforms included the decision to celebrate the Church's liturgy in the vernacular, rather than in Latin as had been the practice for centuries.

Insisting that the richer nations should help the poorer ones, he shocked many westerners by receiving in Rome the son-in-law of the USSR premier Nikita Khrushchev. An equally radical religious event was his reception of the Anglican Archbishop of Canterbury, the first to be honoured in this way since the Reformation. And he went out of his way to remove any anti-Jewish elements from traditional Catholic attitudes and ceremonies.

His successor in 1963, Pope Paul VI, was his devotee. A series of Vatican Council meetings, continuing in the spirit of that inaugurated by John XXIII, particularly emphasised the kinship between different Christian churches, as did Paul VI by his own generous words and actions. Following John XXIII's example, he sought out the Eastern Orthodox Patriarch at Alexandria, as well as again inviting the Archbishop of Canterbury to Rome.

Many of his flock were disappointed that he condemned artificial methods of birth control, even though a commission he had appointed decided in favour of them in some circumstances. In politics he was a close friend of the Italian Christian Democrat leader Aldo Moro, and was deeply distressed at his kidnapping and murder. Paul VI's last public act was to preside at the funeral of his friend.

John Paul I, elected on 26 August 1978, seemed likely to be a remarkable pope. Born of poor, working-class parents who were active socialists, although his views had moved to the right by the time he became pope, he never forsook his radicalism. Even so, he declared that communism and Christianity were incompatible. He also relished literature, publishing entertaining letters to such long-dead authors as Charles Dickens (he adored Mr Pickwick). He also abhorred pomp and circumstance, and his investiture as pope was one of the simplest in history. Three weeks later he was found dead in his bed.

Conspiracy theories abound: that the tainted Vatican Bank arranged his murder; that some of the dignitaries of the papal court feared that he would sack them, and therefore arranged to have him poisoned.

His successor, the first non-Italian pope since Hadrian VI (who reigned in the mid-twelfth century), was born in Poland. The influence of John Paul II has been immense. His support for the freedom movements in eastern Europe was a major contribution to the end of communist tyranny there. Yet John Paul II's commitment to freedom in the political sphere has not been matched by a similar commitment to freedom within the Church he heads. During his pontificate radical theologians have been ruthlessly purged. Critics of his régime find themselves systematically ousted from influence within Catholicism.

Committed in his writings to the rights of working men and women, this pope has nonetheless resolutely opposed those leaders of his Church who have allied themselves with the class struggle. John Paul II has provoked enemies – so much so that he was the victim of an assassination attempt which nearly ended his life. As for his specific religious opinions, they have been consistently conservative, combined with a supreme devotion to the Blessed Virgin Mary.

These eight men have ensured that the papacy has played a more prominent role on the world's stage than at any time since the middle ages and the issues they have confronted remain amongst the most important in the lives of all of us.

Without either idolising or denigrating the papacy, this book seeks to make responsible, independent judgements on the achievements of these influential and saintly men.

James Bentley
June 1977

CHAPTER ONE

The Legacy of Leo XIII

'It is the sure sign of a shallow mind, to suppose that the strength of the Catholic Church is really in its tone of absolute certainty concerning its dogmas, in its air of omniscience,' wrote Matthew Arnold in 1879. 'On the contrary, as experience widens, as the scientific and dogmatic pretensions of the Church become more manifestly illusory, its tone of certitude respecting them, so unguarded, so reiterated, and so grossly calculated for immediate and vulgar effect, will be an embarrassment to it.'

Arnold added, 'The gain today, the effect upon a certain class of minds, will be found to be more than counterbalanced by the embarrassment tomorrow.' Yet, Arnold continued, Catholicism had a great future before it. He believed that it would outlive all the Protestant sects (amongst which he did not include the Church of England). 'I persist in thinking that the prevailing form of Christianity of the future will be a form of Catholicism; – but a Catholicism purged, opening itself to the light and air, having the consciousness of its own poetry, freed from its sacerdotal despotism and freed from its pseudo-scientific apparatus of superannuated dogma.'

Matthew Arnold published these views a year after Leo XIII had been elected pope. When Leo XIII died on 20 July 1903, he had been pope for more than twenty-five years. His pontificate proved Arnold's percipience. It also set the scene for the eight men who followed him in the papal chair throughout the twentieth century. A history of these popes must take into account the legacy of Leo XIII, for any account of the twentieth-century papacy must begin with the legacy of the nineteenth century and of the many problems it created. Few of these problems have yet been solved by the twentieth-century Catholic Church.

No one had expected this pope to live so long. Like Pope John XXIII (elected seventy years later at the age of seventy-seven), Leo XIII had been regarded by many as merely a stop-gap pope. As we shall see, stop-gap popes frequently throw those who elect them into perplexity. Leo XIII's reign proves this rule. Just under sixty-eight at his election and in fragile health, Pope Leo XIII confounded all expectations, living on for another quarter of a century and was aged over ninety when he died. Moreover, he repeatedly changed his mind – sometimes abandoning what Matthew Arnold called superannuated dogma, at other times insisting on certitude.

This pope also brought into focus another problem for his twentieth-century successors, namely the gulf between successive progressive and conservative popes and the difficulties this causes for those well-disposed to Roman Catholicism. Initially, many observers considered Leo XIII a progressive, especially in comparison with his predecessor Pius IX. In this they were half-right, half-wrong. In his encyclicals, Pope Leo XIII attacked not only nihilism (which was reasonable for a pontiff, by his position dedicated to promoting Christianity) but also socialism, freemasonry and communism. At least two of these beliefs – socialism and communism – were acceptable to many Catholics of that era. In this sense Leo XIII was out of touch with his age (though as Ralph Inge, the renowned Anglican Dean of St Paul's Cathedral, would say, a person married to the spirit of one age often becomes a widower in the next). Yet he also emphatically stated that republicanism was as legitimate a form of government as monarchism.

And in spite of attacking socialism, this man was also known as the pope of the workers – particularly after the publication of his encyclical *Rerum novarum*, which was issued in 1891. Though it endorsed private property, *Rerum novarum* also gave due recognition to trades unions and insisted on social justice, workers' rights and a decent wage for everyone. 'Speedily some remedy must be found for the misery and wretchedness which presses so unjustly on the majority of the working classes,' he declared. 'A small number of very rich men have managed to lay upon the teeming masses of the labouring poor a yoke little better than slavery.'

The pope had been influenced by a group of French industrialists and working men, brought to Rome on three pilgrimages by the enlightened French employer and devout Catholic Léon Harmel. Another influence was the German Bishop of Freiburg, who had scandalised his hearers in a sermon which vividly contrasted the condition of the poor and the wealthy and who presided over a group which demanded a living wage for workers. These men alerted the pope to the social problems of the era, and he in turn attempted to alert his flock. In 1893, for example, he told a French bishop: 'Tell your priests not to shut themselves up inside the walls of their churches or their presbyteries, but to go out to the people and to concern themselves wholeheartedly with the workers, the poor and the lower classes.' Yet throughout the twentieth century the social problem was to remain thorny, even more so when, exactly one hundred years after the election of Leo XIII, a cardinal from a communist land was elected pope.

Leo XIII was also dedicated to Christian reunion – but on his own terms. He longed for the Orthodox and Protestant churches to return to the Catholic fold, and showed great sensitivity in his appeals to them, never speaking of non-Roman Catholics as schismatics and heretics. Indeed, he invented a new, non-polemical phrase for those who refused to accept the Roman Catholic Church as the be-all-end-all of Christianity: Leo XIII referred to them as 'separated brethren'.

This pope particularly longed for reunion with the Church of England. From the mid-nineteenth century, Catholicism had prospered in Great Britain, particularly in England. At the age of eighty-five Pope Leo said, 'How thankfully should I sing my *Nunc Dimittis* if I could do anything, even the least thing, to help forward this union.'

Leo's letter *Ad Anglos*, written in 1895, publicly revealed his deep desire that the members of the English established Church might return to the Roman fold which their predecessors had left in the sixteenth century. Some Anglicans were irritated by what they regarded as its patronising tone. Others, such as Mandell Creighton, Bishop of Peterborough, chose to regard it as 'a token of friendliness and Christian sympathy'. Creighton continued:

> intercourse, friendly feeling, and reflection will enable us or our children to remove misunderstanding, to dissolve the veil of sentiment, to go behind the prejudices created by mistakes and misdoings in the past, to separate what is

> accidental and temporary from what is essential, to discover the real importance of the points which keep us asunder, to raise controversy about passion, to discuss principles without being troubled by the thoughts of temporary loss or gain.

So it seemed in 1895 that some *rapprochement* between old religious enemies might be on the horizon. Yet in the same year, when a papal commission declared that the orders of Anglican clergymen were invalid, Leo XIII endorsed its conclusions. Anglican orders, he said, were completely null and void. Naturally, this enormously disturbed Anglicans, and many Anglican theologians of the time – some were much cleverer than the pope's intellectual supporters – fought back. Mandell Creighton himself, for example, a former fellow of Merton College, Oxford, declared of the pope's advisors that 'their ignorance must be exposed and the bubble of their pretentiousness continually pricked.'

In defending their own right for their clergy to be considered true priests of the Christian Church, the Anglicans won the theological dispute, setting out in 1897 their arguments in an encyclical from the Archbishops of Canterbury and York which pointed to the inadequacies of the Roman Catholic reasoning. The intelligent Pope Leo XIII completely ignored this massive rebuttal of his views. Yet he never shrank from making these views clear, particularly his belief that some supreme authority (namely the papacy) was needed for Christendom. 'How is it they cannot see that the Church must have a head?' he asked.

Leo faced other difficulties. Any moves towards reunion were also faced with the prejudices of the Anglican Archbishop of Canterbury E. W. Benson, who was wont to exclaim that he almost believed that Rome was Anti-Christ. Many in the

Protestant wing of the Church of England shared these views, and were furiously opposed to any reunion with Rome.

More, many English Catholics opposed any rapprochement with Anglicans. They deeply resented the way their Church had been treated over centuries by the English Establishment. Faced with such Catholic intransigence, as Lord Halifax (a High Church Anglican and tireless promoter of reunion) acknowledged: 'Let us remember how the Roman Catholic body in England has been treated under the Penal Laws till comparatively recent times. . . . Only as late as the year 1786 a Benedictine, Dom Anselm Botton, was tried at York for his life on a charge of High Treason for converting a girl to the Roman Catholic Faith.'

Leo XIII also had other things on his mind. He was deeply conscious of the fragile nature of the temporal powers of the papacy. In 1871 the Italian army had taken possession of Rome and made it the capital of King Victor Emmanuel. Shorn of his remaining territories (save for the Vatican itself), Pope Pius IX had chosen to regard the Vatican as a prison – his own prison. Leo XIII set out to find some reconciliation with the secular powers that had rebuffed his predecessor. At that time many Italians were vicious in their opposition to the Catholic Church. Leo XIII strove to bring to an end this anticlericalism which he had witnessed at first hand – above all when the remains of his predecessor were translated from their temporary resting place in St Peter's, Rome, to Pius IX's own chosen resting place, in the basilica of San Lorenzo fuori le Mura. As the funeral cortège left the Vatican, crowds of angry men threatened it, hemming in the procession and attacking the coffin with blows and volleys of stones. Vilifying the memory of Pius IX, some even suggested that his dead body should be thrown into the River Tiber.

'If the remains of Pius IX could not be borne through the city without giving occasion to shameful disorders and violent rioting,' Leo XIII lamented, 'who will guarantee that the same criminal violence would not break forth should we ourself appear in the streets in a manner becoming to our station?' In consequence, Leo XIII, like his predecessor, remained a prisoner in the Vatican, not daring even to venture to the basilica of St John Lateran, his own cathedral, where he would one day be interred.

The pathos of the pope as prisoner was displayed on the day Garibaldi died, 3 May 1882, the feast of the Assumption. On that day the public saw for the first time the new apse of the basilica of St John Lateran rebuilt, enlarged and decorated with mosaics and frescoes at the Pope's own expense. Yet, as his biographer Bernard O'Reilly movingly put it in 1887, 'should Leo XIII's carriage appear in the streets, or should he by some stealthy way appear in St John Lateran this day, Heaven only knows the consequences which would follow.'

Yet the man was personally charming, indeed idiosyncratically so (he loved to take snuff, which often blotted part of his white robes). He was also learned. His encyclical *Aeterni Patris* commended the study of philosophy, and in particular the writings of the thirteenth-century Dominican philosopher St Thomas Aquinas. He threw open the Vatican archives to scholars, and he urged Catholics to study the Bible. He was also devoted to the mother of Jesus – seven of his encyclicals exalted her.

Only in his final years did the views of Leo XIII become more rigid. The effects of these views and their consequences were to be seen for many years, and affected the pronouncements of his successors.

In 1893 Leo XIII's encyclical *Providentissimus Deus* affirmed that the Bible was completely and literally true, written 'at the dictation of the Holy Spirit'. In 1897 he outlined new rules of censorship. In 1900 he presented the Catholic world with a new index of books and literature which were either forbidden or to be read only in expurgated versions. In 1902 he set up a permanent Biblical commission, a committee of cardinals and consultants whose task was to monitor the attitude of theologians to the truth of the Bible and to safeguard the authority of Holy Scripture.

His commission was soon in conflict with the Modernist school of Catholic Biblical scholars, who rejected many of the dogmatic assertions made about Holy Scripture in the past. Modernists accepted the Biblical writers suffered the same limitations as other contemporary historians. They wished to reconcile the study of the Bible with the latest techniques of scientific criticism and they believed that science and historical scholarship could be applied to the Gospels without imperilling essential Catholic doctrines.

One leading Modernist, Alfred Loisy, a priest and a professor in Paris, was already incorporating the fruits of modern Biblical criticism in his lectures. Under fire from Leo XIII, Loisy lost his professorship. He was banned from teaching theology and allowed only to teach Assyrian and Hebrew. In 1908 he was excommunicated, a nineteenth-century decision delayed for a decade.

Leo XIII set out to be an ecclesiastical diplomat. There were some successes. He strove valiantly to repair the relationships between the papacy and other great European powers. In 1886 his emissaries managed to bring to an end anti-Catholic legislation in Germany (where Catholics comprised over seventeen-and-a-half thousand out of a population of nearly fifty thousand). As German chancellor, Ludwig von Bismarck had instituted a savage anti-papal campaign known as the *Kulturkampf*, in the hope that by reducing the powers of the Catholics he would bind together behind his policies liberals and conservatives. Immediately on his accession, Leo XIII set about restoring friendly relations with Germany, well aware that Bismarck's policy had only served to alienate not only German Catholics but also many other reasonable men and women.

In France he was less successful. Leo offended French royalists by his support for the Third Republic; and the French persisted with anti-Catholic legislation. 'Every day brings us sad news from that country,' he wrote. 'We detest and deplore the wrong done to the Catholic religion.' Spain proved an easier quarry, and when the Queen-Regent gave birth to a son, Alfonso XIII, she asked Leo to be his godfather and the pope readily agreed.

Outside Europe the Holy Father sought to alleviate hostility to the emissaries of the Holy See: he wrote to the Emperor of China, beseeching his protection for Catholic missionaries; in a letter to the Emperor of Japan he praised his supposed 'provident foresight' in religious matters; and he insisted that Catholics were at home in the United States of America, where 'the influence of the Church has been constantly exercised on behalf of individual rights and popular liberties.'

Leo XIII's vision was far-ranging. He looked beyond Europe, establishing Catholic hierarchies in North Africa, in India and in Japan. He also founded new dioceses in the USA.

In view of these stressful diplomatic manoeuvres and religious initiatives, Leo XIII was agonisingly disappointed when the Italian government managed to have the papacy barred from the first Hague International Peace Conference in 1899. His aim to be an arbiter of peace was thwarted.

These, then, were the problems left unresolved by the papacy as it entered the twentieth century: the social question; the relationship between the Vatican and communism as well as with other twentieth-century secular powers; the question of papal infallibility; ecumenism; the status of the Blessed Virgin Mary; the political role of a papacy in world conflicts; and the tension between traditional faith and modern scholarship. In spite of his manifest gifts, the legacy of Leo XIII to his twentieth-century successors was a Church in many ways in disarray.

In June 1903 Lord Halifax was granted an audience with the pope. Halifax had met Leo XIII in 1895. Now, he recorded, his face was 'perhaps softer and gentler, but his eyes were as bright and quick as ever.' They talked of many things, in particular the reunion of the Churches. 'But it is my dream,' declared the pope, 'what I desire most of all.' Halifax knelt and asked for a blessing, not only for himself but also for the objects he had at heart. The pope blessed him and the audience ended.

Six weeks later, just after noon, Cardinal Serafino Vannutelli arrived at the Vatican in a closed carriage to administer the last rites to the pope himself. At two minutes past four on 20 July, a blindingly hot day, Leo XIII was dead.

The problems he had grappled with were part of his legacy to his eight twentieth-century successors.

CHAPTER TWO

PIUS X

On a dusty little house in Via Reccati at Castelfranco in the Veneto, a plaque declares that here Giuseppe Sarto lived between 1846 and 1850. During the First World War, when battles raged close to the nearby town of Riese, a yet more remarkable notice, this one merely painted in white, fronted another little building with the words, 'Spare this house which belonged to Pius X.' Before the war was over every house in Riese had been occupied; but this one was left alone. Soldiers walked up to it, read the sign and let it be.

Its owner, Giuseppe Melchiore Sarto, had been born here on 2 June 1835, the son of the village postman, cleaner of the town hall (and part-time cobbler, though most weekdays few wore shoes in this poor village) and his seamstress wife. This man became the only twentieth-century pope so far to be officially declared a saint. Curiously too, this saintly pope seems to have made theological judgements of a kind that scarcely any intelligent Christian would try to justify as the twentieth century comes to an end.

Pius X was intransigent about ecumenicism, Biblical scholarship and the relationship of the Vatican to the secular powers of the world, all problems which would continue to harass the papacy throughout the century. He never fully worked out what ought to be the international role of the papacy, and in consequence made gaffe after political gaffe. But in these respects St Pius X also exemplified some of the dilemmas faced by every Christian in this turbulent century.

In specifically Catholic terms, his succession to the chair of St Peter also exemplifies the bizarre nature by which the Catholic Church at that time chose (and in many respects still chooses) the man known as the Holy Father, self-styled and recognised by millions of Christians as the supreme pontiff of Christendom. His career also displays how the most humble may achieve this exalted leadership in the Christian Church and it illustrates the delicate path that the papacy has always trodden between the demands of Church and State – a path that would become immensely more difficult during the reigns of Sarto's successors.

The first son of the postman and seamstress of Castelfranco had also been named Giuseppe, but died after one week. Giuseppe the second, known in the village by the diminutive 'Beppo', was taught first of all by the local parish priest, and went on to win a scholarship at the local school of Castelfranco, a couple of miles away, walking back to his home in Riese every afternoon. As he once observed, 'When I grow up and enter the world, I shall always return here from time to time to sleep in my old room.' And as a child, after his schooling, he would bring in the cow, milk her and then gather wood.

As time passed his father managed to buy a donkey and trap, in which Beppo and his younger brother, Angelo, would ride to school in Castelfranco. In the evenings the future pope would sit beside the donkey as it grazed, while he read and studied the classics.

Thus by birth Pius X, the first of the eight twentieth-century popes, was radically different from the last nineteenth-century pope, for Leo XIII was upper-crust, the son of a lesser noble family from Carpineto in the hilly country south of Rome. His proletarian successor inherited the burdens of Leo XIII and the problems which Leo had failed to solve.

The young man was destined for the priesthood. The local parish priest was convinced of his vocation; but Beppo Sarto's father was poor, and by now he and his wife had five daughters as well as their elder, devout son. Beppo's parish priest, Don Tito Fusarini, helped by petitioning the Patriarch of Venice (himself born in Riese) to grant Beppo a scholarship at the Catholic seminary in Padua. Cardinal Jacopo Monico agreed. Leaving school, Giuseppe Sarto was able to study at Padua till 1850. Academically and spiritually he shone, coming first in every subject at the end of his first term. As his first report put it, 'His mind is quick, his spirit is strong and mature, and his industry is remarkable.' After his first year the heads of all the faculties agreed that he should be nominated *prima con eminenza*.

Each term the citizens of Riese made a collection to help pay for his studies. He himself walked from house to house, collecting their largesse. At the beginning of his second term a sudden crisis almost brought everything to an end. The Rector of the seminary sent the student home, to try to reach his father's bedside before he died of pneumonia. Sarto's mother greeted him, weary herself, for only four days earlier she had borne her husband another son, named Pietro (who was to die within a year). The father of the future pope blessed the young man from his death bed. Apparently Beppo considered abandoning his vocation to care for his widowed mother and her family.

She convinced him not only that it was his father's wish that he be ordained priest but also that she too believed it to be God's will.

At the age of sixteen Giuseppe Melchiore Sarto received the tonsure in the *Duomo* of Asolo. He still knew poverty. His mother paid for his first cassock with the help of the Castelfranco pawnbroker. Giuseppe himself used pawnshops to fund himself as a curate and parish priest – and also to find money to give to those poorer than himself.

He had some strokes of luck. One of the former Italian ladies-in-waiting to Napoleon I generously helped to fund his training for the priesthood. By now an old lady, Signora Loredan-Gradenigo habitually brought together her more distinguished neighbours, including the local clergy, at her house-parties in her villa near Riese. During his vacations Beppo Sarto became a regular member of these meetings, and she became his benefactor.

Giuseppe Sarto was ordained deacon in the spring of 1858 by the Bishop of Treviso. Finally, he was ordained priest in September 1858 at ancient Castelfranco, on the feast of St Joseph of Copertino. After celebrating his first Mass in the parish church of Riese, he received a letter ordering him to begin work as a curate in Tombolo. To one with Giuseppe Sarto's experience of poverty the summons seemed providential. 'Almost all the people of Tombolo are poor,' he told his mother. 'I have always lived amongst poor people, and I am myself poor; I understand them, and I am certain that they will understand me.'

The newly-ordained priest spent eight years as a curate in Tombolo and then another eight as parish priest of Salzano. Tombolo is in the Trentino district of Italy, where the wine is rich and the fields nourish cattle. As curate, Giuseppe lived with the family of a stonemason, before renting his own home and persuading his sister Rosa to come to Tombolo as his housekeeper. He founded a voluntary school, to teach some of the illiterate villagers to read and write, and he instilled Gregorian chant in his church choir, a passion which he had developed in his last seminary years as director of the choir there.

Poor though his parish was, the curate's finances were improving, in part expanded by an even less likely source than Signora Loredan-Gradenigo. A rich Jewish family who spent holidays at Tombolo employed him to teach their children. His preaching skills also brought him money, as he became more and more in demand at important churches. Yet, to the concern of his sister and housekeeper, Rosa, he frequently gave his money away. In 1862, preaching a funeral sermon for the wealthy patroness of the church, Signora Elisabetta Viani, he observed that she dressed simply in black and abhorred ostentation. 'Her home,' he said, 'was a place of hospitality for the poor, and her door was daily open for the needy.' Signora Viani, Sarto concluded, was poor in spirit. She was thus an example not just for the rich but for all Christian believers, not least the future pope himself.

At the age of thirty-two he was appointed to the living of San Bartolomeo in Salzano. His sister Rosa came with him, but since this was a much larger parish, another sister, Anna, also arrived from Riese to help out with her brother's housekeeping. As well as supervising two curates, Giuseppe soon started teaching Gregorian chant again. In addition, he was responsible for overseeing a boys' and girls' junior school, an orphanage and a poorhouse. Finding, as at Tombolo, that many adults were virtually illiterate, the new parish priest soon introduced classes for older persons, too, basing his teaching on simple Catholic doctrine, with particular emphasis on the place of the Virgin

Mary in the devotion of Christians. A peasant by origin, he was an admirable father to the peasants in his flock, in matters both secular as well as spiritual – for instance, he readily ordered the supply of gravel for the community's roads.

His stature in the parish grew enormously because of the unstinting care he gave to his people during the cholera epidemic of 1873. For some time his two sisters and many others in the parish feared for Giuseppe's own health, as his tireless work took its toll. But with the devoted care of Rosa and Anna he recovered, and then characteristically put himself in debt by borrowing money to improve the local hospital.

This extraordinary parish priest was too gifted to expend his talents entirely in the pastoral ministry. In 1875, when he was but forty years old, the Bishop of Treviso, in the Venezia, appointed him chancellor of the diocese and spiritual director of its most important seminary. Giuseppe Sarto is said to have tried to refuse the post, asking to be left as a simple country priest. The bishop refused, but at least allowed Sarto to remain at Salzano until his accumulated salary paid all the debts he had run up as parish priest.

In November Sarto moved to Treviso and his sisters Rosa and Anna returned to their home in Riese. The former parish priest, now given the title monsignor, was one of thirteen canons of Treviso Cathedral, during whose acts of worship he was delighted to discover that Gregorian chant was treasured. Spiritual director of the seminary students was not his only task. In addition he met and taught some of the hundred lay students who attended the seminary. Soon the bishop made this priest of little more than forty years old rector of the seminary, in charge of the training of all those who had been selected as future priests of the diocese.

Sarto was now moving in the higher circles of the Church.

He visited Rome for the first time in 1877, to give Pope Pius IX the offerings of the people of Treviso on the golden jubilee of his ordination. The following year he was made vicar-general of the diocese. A year later he became superior of the canons. And when the bishop died in the same year, Sarto took on the responsibilities of administering the diocese until a new bishop was appointed.

In February 1880 a new pope, Leo XIII, appointed Giuseppe Callegari as the new Bishop of Treviso. Sarto gladly relinquished his role as administrator but accepted the post of chancellor to the new bishop, an energetic reformer who taught his protégé diplomatic skills. Giuseppe first met Leo XIII a year later, when Christians of Treviso joined many others in a pilgrimage to Rome in expiation of the way Roman unbelievers had vilified the mortal remains of Pope Pius IX. His stint as administrator, his piety, his work amongst the poor and his care for the seminarians all impressed Leo XIII, and in 1884, when the diocese of Mantua fell vacant (its bishop had become Archbishop of Udine), he decided to consecrate Monsignor Sarto as the new bishop.

Mantua was a decrepit, difficult diocese. The sore relations between Church and State had aggravated its problems. The Italian State had even forbidden Bishop Rota, appointed in 1871, to live in the city. Even earlier, when Mantua was under the rule of Catholic Austria, the see had been left vacant because the Austrian rulers disputed with the papacy the right to nominate bishops. Mantua had not held a synod of its clergy for two hundred years. Its clerical seminary had been closed down ten years before Sarto arrived.

Reluctantly, Giuseppe Sarto accepted the new task – reluctantly not because of the difficulties, which Leo XIII outlined to him, but because of his own belief that he was unworthy of such a position in the Church. On 15 November 1884, on the eve of his consecration as bishop, Leo XIII presented him with his pectoral cross, garnished with eight huge rubies.

Sarto still needed government permission to occupy the see, and this was given at the end of February 1885. He left Treviso for Mantua in early April. Once more Rosa and Anna Sarto agreed to care for him there, joined later by their sister Maria.

The diocese was in bad shape. Many layfolk never attended church. Few men offered themselves for ordination. In his first year as bishop, Sarto found only one priest and one deacon to ordain. True to his past, the new bishop reopened Mantua's seminary, appealing for both funds and students. He appointed himself rector. Energetically, he toured his 153 parishes, bringing new life to a flaccid part of Catholicism, setting right laxities and corrupt practices, and rebuking those clergy who had fallen into idleness. He loved chatting with the fishermen beside the banks of the River Mincio which washes Mantua. And three years after his consecration he convened a diocesan synod of all his clergy, to try to tackle their problems and the problems of their parishes.

Some problems were insoluble. One blow occurred when the senior priest of Rovere, Don Giovanni Grisanti, became a Protestant. Canon Roberto Ardigò lost his faith altogether and became a passionate advocate of positivism, the empirical philosophy which maintains that knowledge can only be ascertained through science and observation.

In 1891 Cardinal Agostini, Patriarch of Venice, died, and Pope Leo XIII decided that the patriarch's successor should be the Bishop of Mantua. Virtually unknown outside Italy (he had never visited a foreign land), Sarto was nonetheless by now highly regarded by Leo XIII, who made him a cardinal before appointing him Patriarch of Venice, thereby indicating that the honour was a personal one and not related to his new high office.

The problems of Church and State, which had dogged Italian Catholicism for so long, once again reared. Before he could occupy his see, the new patriarch needed the permission of the Italian government, the secular recognition known as the *exequatur*. No *exequatur* was forthcoming. The State protested that the king should have been consulted over the new appointment, since he had inherited from the doges of Venice the right to nominate the city's patriarchs. So, as the Vatican lawyers disputed the matter with the State's representatives, Sarto remained at Mantua. Not until 1894 was the matter resolved. In the meantime his mother died. Sarto wrote the inscription for her tombstone, which observed that she had raised nine children as good Christians.

Francesco Crispi, the Italian premier, was a man of the left, a former revolutionary who had been forced to flee to France in the turbulent mid-century and had returned with Garibaldi when he entered Sicily, where Crispi became Garibaldi's factotum and political secretary. His leader, Garibaldi, was (in the words of G. M. Trevelyan) strongly anti-clerical, though not by temperament anti-religious. He simply 'wished to see the world purified of priests'. Under Garibaldi's leadership, Crispi had been prepared to invade the papal states. Now the senior politician in Italy, he remained vehemently anti-clerical, his government hampering the teaching of religion in schools and continually interfering in episcopal appointments. By the beginning of 1894 Sarto had virtually given up hope of entering his new see. 'Darker and darker, more and more mysterious I find the problem of Venice,' he wrote. Then suddenly, and inexplicably, on 12 September Crispi's government granted the *exequator*, and five days later Giuseppe Sarto was officially appointed Cardinal Archbishop of Venice.

Little love was lost between the Church and those who

adhered to the views of politicians like Crispi, and the Italian left and Italian liberals could not entirely be blamed for distrusting the Church leaders. Sarto himself was hardly diplomatic in the last pastoral letter he wrote as Bishop of Mantua. In it he claimed that he would in his future ministry continue to adhere to justice and love as well as piety and then went on to excoriate the liberals amongst his future Venetian fellow-citizens. Although liberalism proclaimed love and virtue, Sarto fulminated, their true aim was that of a wolf tearing sheep to pieces, and their so-called cleverness was no Godly virtue. He urged his own followers to be proud when they were insulted as intransigent papalists and clericalists. He went on to declare that he would fight against liberalism not behind closed doors but openly. Was this the wisest way to try to heal the rifts between the Church and State in Italy?

These were the public views of the man who soon would set out by train from Treviso to Venice, accompanied by seven hundred supporters. Small wonder that as his boat sailed down the Grand Canal no flags or garlands decorated the city hall. Nonetheless, a few days later the *Sindaco* (Lord Mayor) of Venice was gracious enough formally to pay a call on the new patriarch. Even so, the *Sindaco* continued to ban Church processions across the bridge to the church and shrine of Santa Maria della Salute. Fortunately for Sarto, in 1895 his opponent fell from power, and the new *Sindaco* rescinded his predecessor's vindictive prohibition.

Yet Sarto continued to attack what he perceived as evil secularist societies. The freemasons particularly irked him, especially when in 1895 they publicly rejoiced at the twenty-fifth anniversary of the fall of Rome. He told the Catholic League against Freemasonry that it was serving the family, the nation and the whole of humanity. He also forbade his clergy to visit an 1895 exhibition of art in Venice because one of the paintings seemed to him to offend the Catholic faith. Yet this man was no mere reactionary, and when the first congress of the Catholic Union of Social Studies met at Padua in 1896, Sarto was there, speaking of the duties of the wealthy towards the poor. Though a poor man from a poor family, here as later he never questioned the immutability of the social order: the rich should be generous; the poor should forswear envy and remain patient and resigned, proud that their state mirrored the image of their impoverished Saviour, Jesus Christ.

Poverty was still one of Giuseppe Sarto's virtues, and at Venice he lived in a couple of sparse rooms of the white marble patriarchal palace. He continued to use part of his now amplified income to subsidise poor seminarians, and was not ashamed to beg money from the rich on their and the Church's behalf. He also developed the habit of visiting the city's prisons – a practice which the publicists of one later pontiff presented as something extraordinary. And whereas at Mantua he had befriended the Mincio fishermen, now he enjoyed chatting with gondoliers.

But the man was more forceful than many initially perceived. His passion for Gregorian chant, whose connection with the late-sixth-century Pope Gregory is exceedingly dubious, led him to set up a commission whose remit included the power to ban any music in church services that did not have the commission's (and implicitly the patriarch's) approval. Under the influence of the German priest and musicologist Franz Xaver Haberl, a renowned expert on the music of the Vatican library, the patriarch also came to admire the polyphonic music of the sixteenth-century composer Palestrina, and this too was acceptable throughout his archdiocese. But works of undoubted piety and splendour (such as liturgical texts set to extracts from Gounod's *Faust*) were ruthlessly condemned, as were the humble instruments which often accompanied a village Mass – a prohibition which much distressed many of the less sophisticated in Sarto's flock. Yet Sarto remained convinced that the Mass was not a performance, particularly not a musical concert, but an act of worship. Music had its part in worship, he believed: its role was to instil in the worshipper solemnity and spirituality.

Though some thought otherwise, clearly his humility and gentleness by no means implied weakness. When he became pope, numerous leading ecclesiastics opposed his reforms of church music. They were sternly cut down to size. A less defensible attitude was Giuseppe Sarto's rigid connivance with anti-Semitism. In Mantua the authorities customarily visited both cathedral and synagogue on the birthday of the king. Bishop Sarto strongly objected to the practice, declaring that, if the civic leaders visited the synagogue, they would find the doors of his cathedral firmly closed.

The year of the assassination of King Umberto I, 1900, was also declared by Pope Leo XIII a jubilee year. Sarto recognised the first by a Requiem Mass in St Mark's, Venice and acknowledged the second by a pastoral letter which once again explicitly spoke of the problems of Church and State, even declaring that the Supreme Pontiff had been the victim of treachery by the Italian State. Three years later, in July 1903, the pope was dying. For some time he had seemed utterly weary, his emaciated body almost transparent. Now he had contracted pneumonia. On the day before his death he rallied, dictating letters, working with his long-time secretary of state Cardinal Rampolla, and even composing several verses in honour of St Anselm. The following day he retired to his bed. On 20 July he was dead.

Giuseppe Sarto celebrated Mass at Santa Maria della Salute and then left Venice for Rome for the pope's burial and for the conclave that would elect his successor. For nine days a bell had tolled for the late supreme pontiff. Then his corpse was lowered into its grave. Giuseppe Sarto noticed that one of the bearers had helped to push in the coffin with his foot. The future Holy Father is alleged to have made the wry comment, 'That is how popes are finally treated.'

Sixty-two cardinals arrived at the Vatican to attend and vote at the new conclave. Shortly before the pope's death the secretary to the conclave had himself died. In his place was appointed the ambitious Archbishop Rafael Merry de Val, son of an Englishwoman and her Spanish husband, former Spanish ambassador to the Vatican. Merry de Val had been educated in England, at Ushaw College, and he frequently holidayed in his mother's homeland. Now he followed the cardinals into the Sistine Chapel.

Giuseppe Sarto was not the favourite for the papal throne. The favourite was Cardinal Mariano del Tindaro Rampolla, Leo XIII's secretary of state. Rampolla was a skilled Vatican diplomat, who had gained a measure of success bringing religious reconciliation to Spain, where Catholics were divided between the Carlists (supporters of the Bourbon pretenders to the throne) and their rivals the Alfonsists. Thenceforth his rise was swift. He was summoned to Rome in 1877 to serve Pope Pius IX as secretary of state for Oriental Affairs in the Congregation for the Propagation of the Faith. By 1882 he was papal nuncio to Madrid and titular Archbishop of Heraclia. Rampolla mediated between Spain and Germany during their dispute over the Caroline islands. In 1887 Leo XIII made him a cardinal and appointed him Vatican secretary of state. Their views (no doubt in part owing to Rampolla's diplomatic skills) were seen by many as identical.

But his bid for the papacy failed on account of this same

diplomatic activity. Cardinal Rampolla had offended Austria: he sympathised with France; he sought cordial relations with Russia; he interested himself in the hopes of the southern Slavs, who were the subjects of Austro-Hungary; he encouraged the Church to support democratic aspirations; and he was an avid supporter of the Austrian Christian Social Movement. And Austria was able to veto his election as pope. Bizarrely, in recognition of the services they had rendered in the past to Catholicism, three European powers, Austria, France and Spain (and, some contended, Portugal), possessed this curious right to veto a candidate for the papacy, and were especially keen to do so if he had somehow offended those who ruled one of those states.

This veto was ringed with exceptions – in particular becoming invalid if the prospective pope had obtained over two-thirds of the votes of the conclave of cardinals which had met to choose a new pontiff. It had, of course, no religious or Biblical sanction. But the veto could be effective. Spain had exercised this ridiculous right in 1831, excluding Cardinal Giustiani, who had obtained only twenty-one votes.

Ironically, the forthcoming pope, Sarto, had been allotted the rooms normally occupied in the Vatican by the front-runner Rampolla. Meanwhile a stove at the entrance to the Sistine Chapel was primed to receive the voting papers if no cardinal had received the necessary two-thirds of the vote to be elected pope, so that, with the addition of straw, black smoke appearing from the stove's chimney would apprise the crowds in St Peter's Square that they must remain patient for the next vote.

The first vote gave Cardinal Rampolla twenty-four votes, Cardinal Gotti (superior-general of the Carmelites) seventeen votes, and Cardinal Sarto five, the other votes dispersed among other candidates. Black smoke announced to the crowd that no one had received the necessary majority. On the second vote

Rampolla gained twenty-nine votes, Gotti sixteen and Sarto ten. At this moment, at the behest of Emperor Franz Josef of Austria, Cardinal Kniez de Kozielko Puzyna of Kracow vetoed the election of Cardinal Rampolla as pope. The ambitious Rampolla was incensed. Cardinal Oreglia di San Stefano, dean of the sacred college, declared that everyone must ignore the veto, and Rampolla's followers among the cardinals continued to vote for him. To no avail.

Before one cardinal gained the necessary two-thirds of the total sixty-three votes, there were altogether seven (supposedly secret) ballots. In the third ballot Rampolla gained thirty votes and in the fourth thirty-one. Giuseppe Sarto in the same ballots gained twenty-one and twenty-four. Then Sarto streaked ahead, with twenty-seven votes in the next ballot, thirty-five in the sixth and fifty (against Rampolla's ten) in the final one.

So this man with deep blue eyes and snow-white hair, son of the poor, an intransigent foe of what he took to be the evils of liberalism, became pope. Initially reluctant to stand (declaring to a friend that he would prefer to give up his cardinal's hat and become a Capuchin monk), unable at first to declare that he accepted the election, he finally consented. He took the name Pius, he said, in deference to popes of that name who, he said, 'had defended the Church with strength and gentleness.'

Gentleness, indeed humility, distinguished this pope from his predecessor. No longer were visitors received on their knees. Pius X preferred them to sit down. Many were allowed to throng his modest apartments in the Vatican, especially old acquaintances from the Veneto. And he was a pioneering pope in a curiously humble way. Each Sunday afternoon when he was in Rome, he himself would teach the catechism in the courtyard of the church of San Damaso.

One of his first acts (on 20 January 1904) was to abolish the secular veto on papal elections. And Sarto was generous to Rampolla, appointing his rival for the papacy secretary of the Papal Office and confirming his membership of the Pontifical Biblical Commission, which Leo XIII had founded in 1902. Rampolla kept this important post till his death on 16 December 1913.

The English Catholic apologist and biographer Wilfred Ward welcomed the election of the new pope, as did many others. Leo XIII, Ward wrote, had been no true liberal and he (wrongly) went so far as to assert that Leo's predecessor, Pope Pius IX, 'had more of genuine Liberalism in his composition than his successor.' Ward hoped for a change of heart in Leo's successor. Could the papacy move intellectually and politically into the brave twentieth century?

In fact, as the Church historian and theologian Dr Alec Vidler put it, the first twentieth-century pope, inheriting the problems left unsolved by Leo XIII, imposed on Catholic scholars a theological reign of terror. Contrary to Matthew Arnold's hopes, during the reign of Piux X Catholicism did not open itself to light and air, particularly in the matter of Biblical scholarship. In addition, Protestants and Anglicans survived and even flourished, rejecting an easy rapprochement with Rome. Nor did the Eastern Orthodox Church respond to Roman Catholic blandishments, so that the ecumenical question remained unresolved throughout the reign of Pius X and for the rest of the twentieth century.

Unlike Wilfred Ward, those who had read Giuseppe Sarto's earlier words could have peered more sagaciously into the future. In 1887, in a letter to his Mantuan flock, Sarto had roundly condemned what later became generally known as Modernism, the notion, as he put it, that the Church must adapt itself to the needs of the present era, and that modern Christianity must adapt itself to modern philosophy. And as if he had some presage of his own elevation to the papacy, he had told his Venetian flock that, with regard to the Vicar of Christ, 'there should be no questions, no subtleties, no opposing of personal rights to his rights but only obedience.' When he himself became pope, this is precisely what he demanded.

Thus Pius X must take much responsibility for the problems his pontificate caused. A supreme pontiff who had never travelled abroad was unlikely to respond to the nuances of what was happening in the rest of the world. At the time of his election France, for instance, was undergoing a powerfully radical phase under Emile Combes, its prime minister from 1902 to 1905, who was an implacable foe of Catholicism (though he had taught in Catholic schools and still insisted on accepting the moral teachings of the Church).

His party had confiscated monastic property worth some 1,701 million francs. Combes was a more intransigent man than Sarto, and actively worked for a separation between Church and State. Other French politicians, particularly the young socialist Aristide Briand, were more moderate. Nevertheless, under a bill whose provisions were worked out by Briand, the French State ceased supporting the Church, annulling some forty million francs which it had annually paid, while putting the control and upkeep of local parish churches into the hands of layfolk.

Many French bishops accepted this compromise proposal. Not Pius X, and two of his encyclicals roundly condemned both the bishops' compromises and the French government's actions. In December 1905 the concordat of 1801, which had restored Catholicism as the State religion, was unilaterally renounced by the French government, which also separated Church and State and transferred the Church's goods to associations of lay people. Pius X broke off diplomatic relations with France and steadfastly refused to accede to the pleas of French bishops to do some deal with the lay associations. The French Church was thus independent and materially ruined.

Yet paradoxically, for some time the pope smiled benignly on the movement known as *Action Française* and its scintillating leader Charles Maurras. Maurras was a free thinker, but he regarded Catholicism as an essential element in the civilisation of France. He also was an anti-democratic monarchist, and the popularity of his ideas helped to stifle condemnation of the movement in Rome, as well as delaying the papal condemnation of Maurras's books. Even when they were eventually condemned, Sarto as pope never publicly promulgated the condemnation. Perhaps he was wise, for in France few other lay movements at that time supported Catholicism; but his moderacy contrasts startlingly with his attitude to other French Catholics who wished to follow new paths while (unlike Maurras) remaining loyal to the Church.

In Venice Giuseppe Sarto had headed the Workingmen's Association. But he was no advocate of any revolutionary change. France again provoked his opposition. In 1910 he condemned the *Sillon*, a movement seeking to promulgate an updated concept of the French revolution and to reconcile Catholic and left-wing political views. The *Sillon* group was headed by Marc Sangnier, to whose ideas the pope was at first attracted; but he found abhorrent Sangnier's willingness to embrace inter-confessionalism and to co-operate with those who did not unquestioningly accept papal authority on social questions – as Sangnier himself did not. Pius X felt queasy that Protestants were members of such organisations, and explicitly said so in an encyclical of 1912.

As for Modernism, an attitude to Biblical theology and church history which first surfaced in the writings of nineteenth-century Protestant thinkers, as pope Giuseppe Sarto continued to condemn it: in 1906 in his encyclical *Pieni l'animo*, followed in 1907 by two more uncompromisingly hostile encyclicals, *Lamentabilis sane exitu* and *Pascendi Dominici Gregis*. The Holy Father's words did little justice to the honesty and integrity of Modernists, describing them in 1906 as 'ambitious to be considered learned and goaded by curiosity and pride.' Then, having accused the Modernists of moral faults, he recommended that they abandon their own searchings and return to the philosophy of the medieval Scholastics.

The first of the 1907 encyclicals listed no fewer than sixty-five Modernist propositions which the pope deemed unacceptable. The second dubbed Modernism 'the *résumé* of all heresies'. Pius X followed up these encyclicals with the insistence in 1910 that every priest and would-be priest take an oath renouncing its tenets. Many distinguished Modernist theologians were excommunicated and their books placed on the Vatican index of prohibited publications. Distinguished, zealous, conscientious theologians, considered tainted with Modernism, were excluded from Catholic universities and seminaries. Witchhunts, denunciations, suspicion and distrust proliferated. Senior clergymen spied on each other. Pius X dubbed the Modernists 'miserable wretches'. The Abbé Alfred Loisy, accused and vilified for his Modernist tendencies, with five of his books placed on the index of prohibited works, responded by accusing the Vatican, indeed the pope himself, of fanatical idiocy.

In the light of his reactionary views, it seems odd that Pius X in 1909 set up the Pontifical Biblical Institute, an institution devoted to Biblical studies and run in Rome by the Jesuits. Obviously he intended its work to proceed along the lines he had defined in savaging the Modernists. Equally obviously, in the years after his pontificate, it would blossom in quite different ways.

Meanwhile, Protestantism, many of whose theologians seemed to the pope equally tainted with Modernism, was even more anathema to Pius X, who had no direct experience of the Protestant world. His attitude led to a massive political gaffe, for he enormously offended public opinion in the United States of America by refusing in 1910 to grant an audience to the former president Theodore Roosevelt, on the grounds that Roosevelt intended to address the Methodist congregation in Rome. Pius X similarly offended German Protestants by apparently criticising the Reformation in a eulogy of 1910 on St Charles Borromeo.

Why? Like his master, Pius X's secretary of state Rafael Merry de Val believed that the policy of Leo XIII in seeking compromise with secular states had been a failure. In consequence Pius X was recklessly but also courageously willing to antagonise secular governments: the Italian government immediately on his coronation as pope, by declining to bless the city of Rome and the world from the loggia of St Peter's basilica; the British, by sending Cardinal Vincenzo Vannutelli as legate to Ireland; the Russians, by his concern for the Poles; the Portuguese republic, attacked in an encyclical of 1911 for promulgating a law separating Church and State.

Spring 1913 saw the onset of an alarming illness, but the pope, approaching his seventy-seventh year, recovered. The following year, increasingly aware of tensions between the nations, he asked his assembled cardinals who could protect young lives threatened by war if he, whose ministry was one of peace, could not?

In August 1914 Pius X expressed his profound grief at the outbreak of the First World War. (Asked by the representatives of one nation to bless their arms, he had refused, with the words, 'I bless only peace.') He had long foreseen its coming. Before the month was over, a little after one o'clock on 20 August, he was dead.

Many attributed his death to the outbreak of war, even claiming that he died of a broken heart as a result. The truth is that Pius X had felt unwell on 15 August 1914, the feast of the Assumption. After a couple of days in bed, he seemed to be rallying, welcoming some of his relatives. But on the evening of the 18th he became breathless and feverish. Next morning his condition had deteriorated so much that he consented to receive the viaticum, losing consciousness before the anointing could be completely accomplished. He scarcely ever regained consciousness, as cardinals paid their last respects at his bedside.

On his tomb in St Peter's Rome, are the words:

> Born poor and of humble heart,
> Dauntless champion of the Catholic faith,
> Zealous to restore all things in Christ,
> Crowned a holy life with a holy death.

This epitaph was accurate. Throughout his life Giuseppe Sarto had remained a humble man and an exemplary pastor. As priest, bishop, patriarch and pope he had promoted a revival of church music, the care of the poor and the frequent devotion of the faithful to the sacrament of Holy Communion. Even children, once they reached the age of seven or so, should, he believed, communicate at the altar (previously, the earliest age had been fourteen).

After his death many claimed that through his intercessions miraculous cures had occurred. One couple, honeymooning in Rome, had been given a rosary by Pius X. The bride fell ill, her condition apparently hopeless. Her husband wrapped the rosary round her wrist and she recovered. Some allege that Pius X performed miracles in his own lifetime, curing, for example, a thirteen-year-old boy who was apparently dying of typhus at Caglione in the diocese of Mantua. A married couple were said to have brought their paralysed son to an audience; the pope held the boy in his arms, and suddenly the child jumped down and ran about the room. Pius X himself was convinced that he possessed miraculous powers, in particular the gift of second sight. He also had enormous feet and would happily lend his huge red socks to sufferers from foot ailments: it is said that when they put them on many were cured.

Moves to have Giuseppe Sarto canonised began in 1923. A year later his tomb was opened, and his body examined. His corpse was well preserved; his limbs had remained flexible. Many see this phenomenon as a manifestation of the grace of Christ for the bodies of a considerable number of saints have remained after their deaths free of corruption, as Jesus's own body did in his tomb. Some objected because of Sarto's doctrinaire persecution of the Modernists, but Pope Pius XII was anxious to have his predecessor canonised – no doubt anticipating, wrongly, his own speedy canonisation after his death.

In the Roman Catholic Church canonisation (or sanctification, as it is sometimes called) proceeds by two stages, beginning with beatification, when the Church holds up for public veneration a person who has been martyred or who has led an extraordinarily holy life. Usually veneration is restricted to the territory of a religious order. Canonisation follows, if the Church definitively declares that the person is amongst God's saints and may be publicly venerated throughout the whole Church. In 1951 Giuseppe Sarto was beatified. In 1954, forty years after his death, Pius X was declared a saint, the only twentieth-century pope so honoured and the first pope to be canonised since Pius V in 1721.

CHAPTER THREE

Benedict XV

It behoves a pope to glorify his predecessors. Repeating the pious legend, Pope Pius XII said that the heart of Pope Pius X had been broken by the outbreak of the Great War, adding that his successor, Benedict XV, was still more mortified by the slaughter of nations between 1914 and 1918. According to Pius XII, Benedict XV 'breathed, spoke and prayed for peace.'

This assessment was 90 per cent correct. Yet this pope was vilified in his lifetime and afterwards. Benedict XV, in the words of the Catholic historian Philip Hughes, 'passed into an oblivion as unintelligent as was his wartime unpopularity.' Yet this pope longed to be a pope of peace. 'Without the Church,' he once declared, 'mankind would sink into barbarism.' To him, the Church was the sole institution which contributed to the peace, safety, prosperity and future of all people.

Supremely his reign reveals the difficulties of attempting to pursue these high ordeals, as if somehow the papacy is not tainted with the failings of a fallen world. Peace is not readily achieved, whatever the amount of goodwill. The reign of

Benedict XV also illustrates how any pope can be burdened by the affairs of his predecessors, for this pontiff was ultimately baffled by the problems of Modernism, of ecumenism, of Church-State relations, and (particularly as an aristocrat) of the relationships between the different social classes.

Unlike his predecessor, Giacomo della Chiesa was a scion of the Italian nobility. His mother's family, the Migliorati, had sprung from Cosimo Migliorati di Sumlona, collector of papal revenues in England under Pope Urban VI and himself elected Pope Innocent VII in 1404. His father's ancestors had been equally illustrious, though they made their name as soldiers and statesmen as well as ecclesiastics. Giacomo della Chiesa's father was the Marchese Giuseppe della Chiesa, his mother the Marchesina Giovanna. His elder sister would marry Count Fausto Persico of Venice.

Into this privileged family Giacomo della Chiesa was born at Genoa on 21 November 1854. Physically the future pope was slightly deformed: short, partially lame, his right shoulder higher than his left one. People came to dub him *il piccoletto*, the dwarf, and with characteristic good humour, he himself sometimes used the same name. His forehead was high, topped in his younger days by black hair. His lips were drawn, framing a large mouth.

In his childhood Giacomo displayed unusual piety, a piety which he held to be particular to the Genoese. In 1900, in a prose poem in honour of the Virgin Mary, Giacomo wrote: 'Mary, cherish that integrity of faith which is the greatest pride of the people of Genoa; look graciously upon their devotion and increase in their hearts their zeal for the glory of God.'

Though intended by his father for the study of law, Giacomo soon determined to enter the priesthood. In 1871 he began to study at the royal university of Genoa, gaining his doctorate in civil law in 1875. Then Giacomo reminded his father of his primary vocation. The Marchese astutely suggested that his son prepare for the priesthood not in Genoa but in Rome, and Giacomo accordingly entered the Capranica College there in November of the same year.

In December 1878 he was ordained priest. As no doubt in those days it befitted a man of his social origins, his first Mass was said above the tomb of St Peter in the Vatican basilica. His third Mass was said in yet another major Roman church, Santa Maria Maggiore. Meanwhile his academic studies continued with remarkable success, for in 1880 he graduated as doctor of law with the highest honours. Early the following year he met and was taken under the wing of the formidable Monsignor Rampolla, who was to prove vital in promoting the young priest's ecclesiastical career.

When Rampolla went in 1883 as papal nuncio to Spain, he took with him as personal secretary his young protégé. The two men returned to Rome in 1887, and, when Rampolla was made cardinal and Leo XIII's secretary of state, he appointed Giacomo his under-secretary. The cardinal so much valued the support of Giacomo that in 1901 he successfully pleaded with the pope not to appoint his aide to the archsee of Genoa.

Rampolla was not the only patron of Giacomo della Chiesa. Unlike Pius X, who rose from humble stock, the prestige of the family of Giacomo della Chiesas brought him other important and useful contacts – for example, his father's friend Monsignor Gaetano Alimonda, who was provost of Genoa cathedral and would progress by way of the bishopric of Albenga to become Cardinal Archbishop of Turin. Another patron was a kinsman, Monsignor Lucido Maria Parocchi, successively Bishop of Pavia, Archbishop of Bologna and Cardinal Vicar of Rome.

And his mother was an assiduous advocate of Giacomo's

career, badgering Rampolla to promote her son to some distinguished position in the Church. But after the death of Leo XIII, when Rampolla was replaced as secretary of state by his rival Cardinal Rafael Merry de Val, della Chiesa's star waned. The response to his mother's requests and her son's reward came only in 1907 when Pope Pius X appointed him Archbishop of Bologna.

It seemed an honour. In reality it was a kind of demotion. Almost certainly at that moment della Chiesa desired the vacant post of nuncio to Spain. The Spanish ambassador told him that the job was his. Newspapers had even announced his appointment. The pope personally disabused him, and della Chiesa resignedly wrote to his brother, 'So I'm not to go as nuncio to Madrid, since it has pleased God to have me appointed Archbishop of Bologna.' He told the pope that the tasks ahead frightened him – especially as his predecessor had left the diocese in considerable disorder.

Never one to smile graciously on less well-born folk, nonetheless within four years the aristocratic archbishop had visited every part of his diocese. Many humbler people warmed to him simply because he gave away a lot of money. Sometimes he reached remote mountain villages on horseback. Though not a rich man, his father had been a generous and charitable one, endowing a home for children who had offended the law and setting up an organisation to care for ex-convicts. Giacomo tried to match him in generosity and charity.

He continued to do so till the end of his days, sometimes as pope taking a gold piece from his pocket and tossing it into the air, so that his servants could scrabble for it. So impulsive was he in supporting good works and new, charitable endowments as well as sending money to relieve such hardships as that created by the Russian famine of 1921, that by the time of his death the Vatican coffers were virtually denuded.

When Giacomo della Chiesa first arrived at Bologna, many in his new diocese wondered at his curiously tiny frame. Some faithful Catholics in his diocese also wondered why their archbishop, unusually, had not been made a cardinal. Della Chiesa became a cardinal only in May 1914, a few months before the outbreak of the Great War and the death of Pius X.

As Giacomo della Chiesa reached the conclave which would elect a new pope, many joked about his name, della Chiesa ('of the Church'). Each time the Archbishop of Bologna responded with good-hearted banter. Said one, 'Let the Holy Spirit alight on a cardinal of the Church.' Giacomo replied, 'Let the Spirit do so speedily, so that I can return to Bologna.'

The conclave opened on 31 August. Of the sixty-five cardinals, all but fifteen had been appointed by Pius X. Two from the USA and one from Canada arrived too late to vote. Another five were too ill to attend. Those who came included men from countries now at war, such as Aiden Gasquet from Britain, Désiré Mercier of Belgium, the Archbishops of Munich and Cologne, and the two primates of Austria. Inevitably many observers supposed that nationalist feelings would influence them in their choice of the new pope. At the same time, others noted that the cardinals from the belligerent countries were far outweighed in number by cardinals from other lands.

With Europe at war, everyone was anxious to proceed with the utmost speed. Three candidates emerged as favourites: della Chiesa; Pietro Maffi, Cardinal Archbishop of Pisa; and Cardinal Domenico Serafino. Maffi's problem was his impassioned Italian nationalism, while Serafino was but fifty-one years old and considered by many still too young. There were ten ballots. Late on the hot, sunny morning of 3 September the white smoke announced to the crowds in St Peter's Square that there was a new pope, Giacomo della Chiesa. He took the name of the Bolognese Benedict XIV, who had reigned from 1740 to 1757. Benedict XV gave his blessing of peace from the loggia of St Peter's, while war raged throughout Europe.

His dwarf-like frame, with its large head and one shoulder higher than the other, had confounded the Vatican tailors, who had prepared three sets of papal robes, all of which were too large. Physical frailty, however, by no means implied a lack of mental steeliness. The new pope took his revenge on Merry de Val by instantly throwing him out of his prestigious Vatican apartments, replacing him as secretary of state by Cardinal Ferrata. Equally speedily, he asked for information about the finances of the Vatican and he decided that his coronation would not be a glamorous affair in St Peter's, but a low-key one in the Sistine Chapel, for splendour and Europe at war did not seem to him to go fittingly together.

Five days later, properly dressed, Benedict XV issued an exhortation to the world's faithful Catholics, speaking of his horror and grief at the monstrous vision of war and imploring the rulers of the warring nations to lay aside their differences, to consider the havoc already created and the blood already shed, to engage in counsels of peace and join hands in friendship. This was the entire theme of his papacy.

Benedict XV's first encyclical, issued on All Saints' Day, 1914, was even more uncompromising:

> Undoubtedly those days seem to have come upon us which Christ Our Lord foretold: 'You shall hear of wars and rumours of wars, for nation shall rise up against nation and kingdom against kingdom.' On every side the dreaded

> spectre of war rules; in the minds of the people there is hardly space for any other thought. As for the combatants, these are the greatest and wealthiest nations on earth. Small wonder then, lavishly provided with the most frightful weapons devised by modern military science, that they endeavour to destroy each other with the subtlest horrors. There is no limit to the extent of ruin and slaughter. Each day the earth is drenched with newly-shed blood and covered with the bodies of the wounded and slain. As we observe the nations, so filled with hatred of each other, who would conceive that they share one common stock, that all share the same nature, that all are members of the same human society? Who would perceive that they are all brothers whose Father is in heaven?

He added that daily the toll of widows and orphans increased and that trade and agriculture had virtually ceased. The poor, he declared, were in misery, and even the rich in difficulty. The new Holy Father insisted that there were other means than war to solve the violated rights of nations. He spoke, he said, without any personal interest whatsoever.

Deeply sympathetic to the plight of those suffering in the Great War, the pope persuaded Switzerland to give shelter to soldiers suffering from tuberculosis and he set up a missing persons' office in the Vatican, aimed at uniting prisoners of war with their families.

If Benedict XV hoped that his evident charity and his All Saints' Day protestation would earn him the thanks of the warring nations, he was grievously mistaken. He was even forced to close his missing persons' office under the accusation that it was a cover-up for spies.

The problem was that each side desired his support. That he

refused to be a partisan enraged all the belligerents. When in 1914 the pope appealed for a Christmas truce, one by one the leaders of the warring nations found reasons to demur, each side at this time confident of victory without any surrender. In 1915 the pope composed a prayer for peace. The French government forbade any public recitation of his petition. When the pope strongly disapproved of the German invasion of Belgium, the Prussian minister to the Holy See sent in a formal protest. Benedict alienated the Germans by condemning the sinking of the liner *Lusitania*. He annoyed the French by refusing to condemn Germany entirely (Georges Clemenceau, at that time premier of France and an implacable foe of Germany as well as a man of the left, is said to have dubbed him the 'Boche pope'). In truth, he was virtually a pacifist in relation to the First World War, never, for instance, allowing any army chaplain to appear in his presence in a military uniform.

Throughout his pontificate, Giacomo della Chiesa repeatedly condemned what he described as the horrible carnage that was tantamount to the suicide of civilised Europe. The war, he insisted, displayed the darkest tragedy of human hatred and madness. In January 1914 he entreated the belligerent nations to allow home all those who had been interned, including women and children, youths under the age of seventeen, adults aged over fifty-five, doctors, clergymen and all those who were disqualified for military service. This was a humanitarian gesture that few could criticise. Yet in vain did the belligerents look to him for any open condemnation of the aggressors, not even of the Germans for violating the neutrality of Belgium.

And Benedict XV was not entirely impartial in his political views. In particular, he deplored British policy towards Ireland. Unanimously, the Irish Catholic bishops were opposed to conscription imposed by the British government, and the pope supported them. To the British government the introduction in 1915 of the cause for the beatification of 257 Irish martyrs of the sixteenth and seventeenth centuries could only appear provocative.

On 1 August 1917 Pope Benedict XV issued his ill-fated peace note. Delivered by nuncios to every government with which the Holy See had diplomatic relations, transmitted in other ways to the rest, it was accompanied by a covering letter in which Cardinal Gasparri declared that the Holy Father, desiring to do everything possible to end the conflict that for three years had ravaged the civilised world, was setting out concrete propositions for peace. In his note the pope affirmed (perhaps mistakenly in view of the passionate politics involved in the war) his absolute impartiality to all the belligerents. He insisted that he had no private, political aim.

Then he declared, 'The moral force of right ought to be substituted for the material force of arms.' Therefore the war should immediately end. Next, armaments should be mutually reduced, each state retaining only sufficient weapons to keep order within its borders. And some instrument of arbitration needed to be found, able to impose sanctions on any nation that refused to accept the decisions of international arbitration. Over territorial disputes, the various parties ought to become conciliatory. Armenia, the Balkans and the former kingdom of Poland all needed special consideration. Economic problems must be tackled. Above all, a solution had to be found which would render similar conflicts impossible in the future.

Scarcely anyone regarded the pope's proposals as remotely feasible. Georges Clemenceau, for example, derided the note. The Germans responded more courteously – but also equivocally – thanking the pope for his zeal for humanity but at the same time refusing to agree to his plea for Belgium's independence. By contrast, the Italian State, with brutal discourtesy, brusquely rejected the pope's views. And when the war was over the Roman Catholic scholar and writer Baron von Hügel told Alfred Loisy that in his view not only Kaiser Wilhelm II but also Pope Benedict XV ought to abdicate.

Others accused this supreme pontiff, who had striven so scrupulously to remain neutral, of being an ally of Catholic Austria. He was described as pro-German, as a supporter of the Entente, as an unduly prejudiced friend of Belgium. An astute English Catholic, Masie Ward, put her finger on the pope's problem; he was, she wrote, simply 'pro-peace'.

But his seven-point proposal was indeed flawed. It was biased in favour of Germany. Perhaps the pope leaned that way because the German authorities had promised to give Rome back to the Holy See after defeating Italy. Perhaps too he feared an expansion of Eastern Orthodoxy in the event of an allied victory.

Nothing he did seemed acceptable to nations at war. In 1915 Pope Benedict XV had composed a prayer for peace, which included the words, 'Dismayed by the horrors of war, O Jesus we turn to your most loving heart as our final hope. O God of mercy, tearfully we beg you to end this fearful scourge. O King of peace, we humbly beseech you for the peace for which we so long.' Benedict ordered that this prayer should be used alongside the exposition of the Blessed Sacrament in every European Catholic church on Sexagesima Sunday (which fell on 7 February) and in every church throughout the rest of the Catholic world on Passion Sunday (which fell on 21 March). His plea greatly annoyed the belligerents, so much so that the French government forbade any public recitation of his prayer.

His scrupulous neutrality (save in the matter of Ireland and his unfortunate apparent support of Germany) caused outrage on other occasions. When Austrian aeroplanes bombed the undefended city of Padua, killing scores of people, he telegrammed the city, deploring and condemning such aerial bombardments of inoffensive places, 'by whomsoever they were carried out.' Benedict also sent ten thousand Lire to help the distressed. But in his telegram he did not name Austria and for this he was vilified by Austria's enemies.

Ironically, then, because of his tireless wartime activities to bring an end to the carnage, this pro-peace pope was excluded from any part of the peace negotiations that ended the war. All he could do was declare that those who were faithful to him would back any attempt to bring about a peace that was just. And in the post-war years, anxious to reconcile the nations that had fought bitterly for so long, he insisted that both the French and the German ecclesiastical hierarchy abandon nationalism and embrace each other.

His views were still robust. In 1920 the Versailles treaties earned the condemnation of his encyclical *Pacem Dei munus*. The League of Nations he found contemptibly weak.

Poland and the Ukraine also concerned him. To the latter he sent Fr. Giovanni Genocchi as apostolic delegate. As for Poland, with the success of the Bolshevik revolution this land seemed one of the last bastions against communist atheism. In the eyes of Benedict XV, a hateful propaganda was seeking to steal the Catholic faith from the children of that country. The pope sent as his envoy to the beleaguered country Achille Ratti, the man who would succeed him in the Holy See. When Poland seemed doomed and the envoys of the great powers fled, only one remained to face whatever was to come: the papal nuncio.

Communism was not the only political theory that Giacomo della Chiesa deplored. In his view, socialism, too, was anathema, no doubt in part because its Italian forms were (unlike those, say, in Britain) materialist. There could be no hope for social prosperity or human happiness from mere humanitarianism, he taught, unless it was inspired by Christian principles.

Evidently, the conspicuous charity displayed by Giacomo della Chiesa by no means implied any revision of the social and economic order. His first encyclical, *Ad beatissimi*, issued on All Saints' Day 1914, deplored the secular cast of many minds in the twentieth century. It seemed to him that the relationships of mutual love had disappeared from society. Not only that: a spirit of insubordination was rife. 'The authority of rulers is held in contempt,' he wrote. To this he (not quite logically) attributed other social evils. 'Between the classes of society injustice reigns; people keenly strive for the transient and perishable, losing sight of other, worthier goods.' Benedict's view of the proper relation between the classes was further spelled out when he condemned the 'insubordination of the masses, their wanton criticism of orders issued by their superiors and the consequent innumerable ways in which authority is undermined.' He particularly criticised those who attacked 'the property and the lives of their fellow men'.

Small wonder that this aristocrat who supported a hierarchical structure in the social order also fervently defended his own authority as pope and the hierarchical structure of the Church. Among the clergy, Benedict XV declared, 'The spirit of insubordination to bishops is the equivalent of resisting God.'

In some of his endeavours, the pope was successful. Secularised France proved easier than the communist world to reconcile to the Holy See. On 16 May 1920 the pope canonised St Joan of Arc, at a ceremony attended by some eighty members of the French parliament. Next, his legate in Paris raised with Aristide Briand's government the possibility of resuming diplomatic relations with France. On 30 November the French government approved, by 391 votes to 179.

The legacy of his two predecessors, Leo XIII and Pius X, with regard to the kingdom of Italy also weighed heavily on Benedict XV. Even while condemning the Great War, the pope had been moved to draw attention to the Roman question. For many years past the Church, he lamented, had not enjoyed the full freedom it needed, not since the supreme pontiff was deprived of 'that protection which Divine providence had set up over the ages.' Benedict added that all who professed themselves children of the Roman pontiff should demand a guarantee that in the performance of his holy office he should be completely free from all human powers. 'And so,' he concluded, 'while earnestly desiring that peace be concluded amongst the nations, we also desire that the abnormal position of the head of the Church be brought to an end – a position in many ways harmful to the very peace of the nations.'

Despite these fine words, relationships between the Vatican and the Italian government proved far more difficult to ameliorate than those between the papacy and France. In its antagonism to the papacy, the Italian government had been determined that when the moment came to negotiate a peace treaty at the end of the First World War, no papal representative should take part. Benedict XV did his best to improve matters, for instance softening the hard line of his predecessors by instructing the heads of state of Catholic countries to pay official respects to the Italian king.

He also softened his predecessors' attitude to the Modernists. Benedict's very first encyclical, *Ad beatissimi Apostolorum Principis*, still condemned these Catholic scholars. For the most part, he merely repeated the anathema of Pope Pius X: 'Our predecessor rightly declared that Modernism was the résumé of all errors. We hereby renew that condemnation in all its fullness.' For Benedict some words of the book of Job seemed entirely apposite to the creed of the Modernists: 'It is a fire that consumes unto destruction and would root out everything that grows' (Job 31, verse 12).

But then he rounded on the more savage of the Modernists' opponents. They should refrain from excessive rancour in their speeches; they should remember the Pauline injunction to charity; they should at the very least be courteous to those who held different theological views from their own.

As for ecumenicism, as his own decrees showed, Benedict XV's attitude was some fifty years out-of-date. In 1919 he issued a decree confirming the decree of 1864 which forbade Catholics to take part in any meeting or society aimed at promoting the unity of Christendom by recognising non-Catholic Churches as branches of the one true Church. Protestants, he believed and specifically declared, were the emissaries of Satan.

But in spite of these harsh words, even now, as with the Modernists, the Holy Father contrived to sit uncomfortably on the fence. He vacillated. Perhaps ecumenical relations might bring back Protestants under the umbrella of Rome. So when Cardinal Mercier of Malines and the Anglican high churchman Lord Halifax set up conferences on the problems that divided the two communions, Benedict XV did not ban them and even gave them his qualified approval.

On 21 November 1921, an extremely cold day, he was delayed outside the basilica of St Peter's, and developed influenza which led to bronchitis. Benedict XV seemed unable to shake off this sickness. Early in 1922 the pope was increasingly beset with fits of coughing, yet at first he refused to believe that his illness was terminal. He was still imbued with passionate notions of the expansion of the Catholic Church – in China; in the Islamic Middle East; in the philosophical world through a revival of Thomism; and in the world of the Catholic laity by allowing laymen to study in prestigious papal academies. Benedict XV clearly had no intention of dying just then. The pope was a mere sixty-seven years old.

When, early in January, his courtiers, his relatives and his friends told him that outside his apartment men and women were praying for his survival, Benedict XV could scarcely believe it. On 8 January Cardinal Gasparri came to meet him for his customary early morning audience, only to learn that the pope had not yet risen from his bed. Finding Giacomo still languishing in his bedroom, Gasparri persuaded the pope to postpone that day's meetings. Evidently the pope was dying, though none (least of all himself) wished to admit it. Soon Benedict XV's shortness of breath became intense. Influenza and bronchitis became pneumonia. By Sunday morning, 22 January, the pope's life was clearly at an end. The death rattle gurgled in his throat. His face grimaced in pain. At six o'clock in the afternoon he was dead.

A future pope, Battista Montini, then a student in Rome and like Benedict XV born into the upper crust, joined the throng that viewed the dead pontiff, whose corpse, dressed in red pontificals and a mitre encrusted with gold, was laid out in St Peter's basilica, in the chapel of the Holy Sacrament. 'His wax-like face, pale, angular and emaciated, still expresses his character, the black hair tumbling over his brow,' Montini wrote. 'He is dead, his right hand lying inertly upon his august breast as if weary from blessing.'

CHAPTER FOUR

Pius XI

Benedict XV had died unexpectedly and in 1922 the cardinals assembling in Rome had little time to plot amongst themselves or negotiate who should succeed him.

The previous year, on 13 June, the late pope had given a cardinal's hat to Achille Ratti, Archbishop of Milan. Benedict XV described the two-fold achievements of his new cardinal: as scholar and librarian, and as diplomat of tact and unruffled calm in dangerous, difficult times. The pope had scarcely six months to live, and Achille Ratti was to enjoy little more than six months as Cardinal Archbishop of Milan.

Just before his train left Milan railway station for the conclave to elect a new pope, Ratti said, 'I bless Milan and wish to come back here.' He never saw Milan again.

Apart from Ratti, two other men were favourites as *papabili*: Cardinal Merry de Val, formerly secretary of state to Pope Pius X, and Cardinal Gasparri, the late Pope Benedict's secretary of state. Three days after the conclave opened, neither had obtained the necessary two-thirds majority of the votes. Another candidate was canvassed, La Fontaine, Patriarch of Venice. Gasparri had received an inadequate twenty-four votes; La Fontaine gained only twenty-three.

Cardinal Ratti so far had received only five votes, but now his star began to ascend. One reason was that Gasparri, having failed to be elected pope, now began to promote Ratti's cause, secure in the promise that if his protégé became pope Gasparri would be appointed his secretary of state. In the next four ballots Ratti received eleven, twelve, twenty-four and twenty-seven votes. Finally the second ballot of 6 February (the fourteenth ballot of the conclave) gave him forty-two votes, and at 11.45 a.m. white smoke announced his election. Cardinal Bislati appeared before the massed crowd in St Peter's Square and announced that the new pope was the former Archbishop of Milan.

For a second time the unfortunate Cardinal O'Connell, the Archbishop of Boston, arrived, as he had done so for the conclave that elected Benedict XV, too late to vote. This time he made his views clear, politely but firmly, to the new pontiff. As conditions were, cardinals from the United States would be for ever excluded from the sacred right of electing a new pope. Pius XI listened, and in 1922 decreed that ten to eighteen days should henceforth elapse between the death of a pope and the election of his successor.

He took the name Pius because, he said, he had been ordained priest under Pius IX and called to Rome by Pius X. Then he made a small but momentous decision: to bless the people assembled in St Peter's Square, the whole of Rome and the rest of Italy from the outer loggia of St Peter's for the first time since 1870. The pope's blessing *Urbi et Orbi* was a sign that Pius XI no longer wished to live as the prisoner in the Vatican. Thus this new pope, whose experience was almost entirely that of a scholar, with a little experience as a papal diplomat, had made a gesture of conciliation to the Italian State. As a reciprocal gesture of recognition, troops of the Italian army responded by presenting arms.

Pius XI proved an extraordinary mixture as pope. This man was a scholar now plunged into a bewildering world of diplomacy. Unlike most of his predecessors, he was a friend of scholars in Protestant lands and had frequently visited many of them, yet he remained obdurately opposed to any concession by Rome to either Protestant or Orthodox churches. As pope he lived in the era of the dictators, and he was willing to make alliances with them. And yet, at the very end of his life, he delivered a stinging rebuke to one of the most fanatical of them all.

But first he flooded the Vatican with his friends from Lombardy, not simply priests and ecclesiastical bureaucrats but also the builders of a Milanese entrepreneur, Leone Castelli. Castelli's firm strenuously renewed and in part transformed both the Vatican apartments and a good deal of Castel Gandolfo.

The successor of Benedict XV as pope had been born at Desio, not far from Milan. Unlike those of his predecessor, his parents were not aristocrats but peasants, cotton-spinners, though the future pope's father had risen to be manager of a silk factory. The child was their fourth son, and his mother was to bear her husband another son and one sister. They baptized their fourth child Ambrose Damien Achille.

Taught at first by the local parish priest (since Desio had no school), inspired by the learning of his genial uncle who was a parish priest at Pieve di Aso near Lake Como, Achille, as he was habitually called, went on to study at the college of St Charles Borromeo in Milan, where he was regularly awarded the medal of that saint presented to the best student in the college. Achille was so proficient in the natural sciences and mathematics that initially he hoped to move on to the University of Turin to study the latter.

His devout mother thought otherwise. She petitioned the Archbishop of Milan, the remarkable Monsignor die Conti di Calabiana (who had reaped some obloquy by voting against papal infallibility at Vatican I and thus never gained a cardinal's hat), persuading him that her son should continue his studies in Rome. In the autumn of 1879 Achille obediently went on to Rome to study canon law at the Lombard seminary.

In the same year the young seminarian was ordained priest in the Basilica of St Giovanni Laterano, and three years later he had three degrees: one in canon law, a second in philosophy and a third in theology. The philosophy of St Thomas Aquinas was at that time supreme in Catholic eyes, and when Achille and two other students were privileged to be given an audience with Pope Leo XIII, the pope urged them to promulgate it. The young man again obediently studied Thomism at an academy founded by Pope Leo himself.

Achille was destined to teach, and after a short time as curate, he returned to the theological seminary in Milan, this time to instruct younger men. His post brought the cotton-spinners' son into contact with some of the most influential families of the city, many of them if not liberal then certainly moderate in their political views.

At this time Achille Ratti was an enthusiastic mountaineer, a member of the Alpine Club who scaled Monte Rosa by the eastern wall in 1889 (the first Italian to do so), ascended the Matterhorn from Zermatt and conquered Mont Blanc. High on these peaks Achille felt himself close to God. 'One can but pray here,' he exclaimed on Monte Rosa. 'We felt we were present at a novel, immensely imposing revelation of the all-powerful majesty of God.' Ten years later, on 31 December 1899, as the new century dawned, the future pope and some of his friends were at the summit of Mount Vesuvius, waiting for the first light.

In 1888 a new post had become available, as one of the curators of the Milan Ambrosian Library. Achille applied for the job, won it and remained there for thirty-one years. His erudition was vast. He published three scholarly volumes on the history of the Church of Milan since the time of St Charles Borremeo until 1797. These were complemented by a corpus of other scholarly works, as well as more popular ones, such as a visitors' guide to the library. Not surprisingly, when the head of the library died in 1907, Achille took over in his place. Throughout this long period he was working on an edition of the important Milanese liturgy, whose Mass differed in several significant ways from the Roman rite, and in 1913 published an edition (alas incomplete) of this ancient missal.

These were years of considerable political and religious tension in Italy. Archbishop Andrea Ferrari, who succeeded Calabiana in 1894, vehemently opposed the Italian State. When the monarch arrived in his diocese, Ferrari ostentatiously left Milan. Presaging his later stance as pope, Achille Ratti did not share these extreme views. He accepted a prestigious award from Vittore Emanuele III for his scholarly work. He said a Mass for the soul of King Umberto I after the king's assassination at Monza in 1900. Ratti was no liberal, but he was a healer and reconciler.

Such a scholar, however tolerant, was inevitably also forced into a stance on Modernism. After all, he lived in Milan, where the intellectuals (not to mention the great musicians and dramatists) of contemporary Italy predominated. Yet Achille Ratti for the most part kept his views to himself. Even so, as a Thomist,

Ratti could not have been a Modernist, or even a sympathiser with Modernism. Both as Achille Ratti and as Pius XI his views remained the same: the error of Modernism was to insist that, 'dogmatic truth is not absolute, but relative, having to be measured to the different needs of times and places, and to varying trends of thought.'

In 1911 Achille's scholarly zeal was rewarded with the post of deputy-librarian at the Vatican, though he still continued to work as director of the Ambrosian Library in Milan. His researches took him abroad, particularly to Oxford and the Bodleian, to the British Museum Library and to the John Rylands Library in Manchester. He was a welcome scholar in the great libraries of Germany, as well as those of Budapest and Prague. In 1914, during the Oxford celebrations of the seven hundredth anniversary of the birth of the English Franciscan philosopher, Roger Bacon, Achille gave an address on behalf of the Vatican. And in the same year he was appointed a canon of St Peter's, Rome, and director of the Vatican library, whose catalogue he was extensively updating.

This austere priest not only understood Greek, Latin and Hebrew but was also proficient in German (in which he frequently heard confessions). Germany in truth had a special place of affection in his heart. In 1900 he took the trouble to see the Oberammergau Passion Play. He relished German-speaking scholars, such as the historian Ludwig von Pastor, who dedicated the ninth volume of his history of the papacy to the pope (fittingly, since that volume dealt in part with the life of St Charles Borromeo of Milan).

In Rome this scholarly, sturdy man was increasingly in the presence and counsels of Pope Benedict XV, and the latter was increasingly impressed with Ratti. In March 1918 the pope startled the scholarly priest by deciding to send him on a totally new career, as Apostolic Visitor to Poland and Lithuania. The pope was responding to an appeal by the Polish bishops for help with the restoration of the Church in a nation which the soon-to-be-victorious allied powers had determined should become independent – after years of partition between Russia, Germany and Austria. When Achille arrived in Warsaw at the end of May 1918 Germany and Austria were still occupying the capital.

Because of the mutual hostility of the Vatican and the Russian Orthodox Church, many bishoprics in Poland had long been left vacant and some had even been suppressed. Orders of monks and nuns had been abolished. Part of Achille's task was to restore them. Yet in spite of (and perhaps because of) these depredations, the Poles had preserved a fervent sense of the significance of the Catholic faith.

Polish piety was particularly on display when Achille arrived, since he came on the feast of Corpus Christi. On that day the Sacred Host was carried through the streets, and the Archbishop of Warsaw gave the pope's newly-arrived emissary the privilege of carrying it through the capital and four times ritually blessing the people and the city. Poles knelt in their thousands as he passed. Achille next took the opportunity of visiting the celebrated shrine of the Black Virgin of Jasna Gora, near Czestochowa, where again the deep devotion of the crowds praying there immensely impressed him. The Black Virgin of Czestochowa is an icon depicting Mary and the infant Jesus, traditionally said to have been painted by St Luke on a wooden table made by St Joseph on behalf of the home of the Holy Family in Nazareth. More likely, this icon was created in the ninth century, with some thirteenth-century overpainting. It hangs in a basilica outside Czestochowa, on Jasna Gora, which means the hill of light. (After this visit Achille kept an image of the Black Virgin, finally giving it a place of honour in his papal chapel.)

But although he came ostensibly as a religious envoy, he was deeply aware of the political tensions. Poland had been partitioned, and its Church still supported three episcopates instead of one. Russians, Germans and Austrians were now competing for Polish sympathy, even though the first two nations had been in the past particularly hostile to Polish national aspirations. Even more galling was the refusal of the Church authorities to let the pope's visitor (who though a monsignor was not a bishop) join in many of the ecclesiastical sessions.

And the divorce between religion and politics was scarcely sustainable in the most minor ways. Achille came with money given by the pope for dispersion to the poor. Monsignor Achille Ratti noted that many of the starving were Jews, and accordingly did his best to support them as well as the Catholics of Warsaw. He also noted how sad the long liturgical worship of the Polish faithful seemed.

In addition, his mission achieved the restoration of three Catholic sees and the appointment of new auxiliary bishops to assist the Archbishop of Warsaw. When the war ended in November 1918 Monsignor Achille Ratti's work was further complicated, for the newly-elected Socialist and Popular parties deprived the Polish bishops of their seats in the senate. Benedict XV tried to shore up his apostolic visitor's prestige by elevating Achille to the rank of papal nuncio, and in June 1919 appointed him Archbishop of Lepanto. The Archbishop of Warsaw consecrated Ratti in the city's cathedral.

For two-and-a-half years Archbishop Ratti toiled in Poland. One of his major achievements was to persuade the Polish Diet to agree to a concordat with Rome. This concordat was finally signed in 1925, when the man who had helped to draw it up was no longer the Archbishop of Lepanto but Pope Pius XI. He also persuaded the authorities in Riga, the capital of Latvia, to agree to a concordat with the Holy See, this one signed when he was pope in 1922. Achille Ratti was learning diplomacy, which he would test to its utmost during the years of the dictators.

The Russians, now under their own dictatorship, decided to invade Poland. Almost miraculously, under General Józef Pilsudki the Polish forces managed to hold back the Bolshevik army. Poland and Russia signed an armistice in 1920 which was ratified by the treaty of Riga the following year. Pilsudki was not, however, an entirely congenial leader in Ratti's view. A socialist, after a period in retirement in 1926 he became dictator of Poland and continued to rule the country as minister of war from 1928 until his death in 1935. Yet he was charismatic; he was opposed to Russia; and he had no instinctive love of the Orthodox Church. These three traits appealed to Achille Ratti. But he and Pilsudki were never allies.

In Poland Archbishop Ratti had another trial to contend with. In 1918 the Poles issued a claim to the mining country of Upper Silesia, where two thirds of the population were Polish and the rest German. A plebiscite was arranged, and Ratti was asked to help oversee it. When he urged moderation on both sides, both Germans and Poles turned against him. He was further attacked for not preventing the Cardinal Archbishop of Wroclaw from prohibiting his clergy to vote in the elections (on the grounds that this was a secular, not a religious matter).

When the plebiscite favoured the Germans, both the cardinal archbishop and the papal nuncio were viciously attacked by the press. Only two votes stopped the Germans voting to have Ratti expelled from Poland. The pope moved swiftly to protect his nuncio, first making Ratti titular Archbishop of Adana and then the Archbishop of Milan. Achille Ratti reluctantly accepted that his years as a scholar were over and resignedly gave away his own collection of scholarly books.

The post carried with it a cardinal's hat. It also brought political problems, for fascism was increasingly establishing itself in the city, and here Benito Mussolini had set up his headquarters. Mussolini promised law and order, an end to communism and an end to liberalism. His was a programme attractive to many in the Catholic Church, both clergy and laity alike. In Milan Achille Ratti had little time to come to grips with such problems. Five months later he was pope.

On his election, before he appeared on the outer balcony of St Peter's to bless a crowd which stood in a miserably cold February drizzle, he told his fellow cardinals in the Sistine Chapel that he planned to continue his predecessor's search for peace. He would, he added, safeguard the rights of the Church and the Holy See. These were vows that would test him to the uttermost.

Although he was tolerant of the Italian State, Pius XI remained far less conciliatory to communism outside Italy. Soviet communism was persecuting and even executing Christians, including bishops and priests. A papal mission to the USSR was continually frustrated in its attempts to bring charitable relief to Christians there. In 1922 the pope's representatives begged the mostly futile Genoa conference to support in Russia not only freedom of conscience and religion but also the right to own private property. Still in 1930 he was urging in vain that the Soviet leaders stop persecuting religion.

Socialism seemed to him almost as reprehensible as communism. 'No one,' he once asserted, 'can be a good Catholic and a believing socialist.' In his view socialism and anarchy went hand in hand. Egoistic individualism was equally indefensible as socialist collectivism, he declared in 1931 in his encyclical on reconstructing the social order (*Quadrogesimo anno*). And here as always he upheld the right to own private property as God-given. Pius XI worked out a hierarchy of social and political evils. Liberalism was the source of error, he believed; socialism worse; but, as the pope declared in his encyclical *Divini Redemptoris*, 'Communism is intrinsically evil, and no one who wishes to preserve Christian civilization must collaborate with it in any field.'

Mexico caused him similar anguish. Plutarco Elías Calles, president from 1924 to 1928, was a socialist, freemason and fierce anti-cleric. Aiming to wipe out Catholicism in Mexico, he was strenuously opposed by the pope's instruction that Mexican bishops and clergy indulge in no political activity, so as to give the Mexican authorities the least possible ground for persecuting the Church. In Spain, too, anticlericalism was rife. The Jesuits were expelled. After the revolution of 1936 priests and Catholic laymen and women were put to death. Church property was confiscated, monasteries and churches laid waste. Pius XI vigorously protested against the violation of the Church's rights and urged his followers to stand firm.

In his own country he was faced with a dilemma: the fascist march on Rome which in his first year as pope made Mussolini the dictator of Italy. Here the pope decided to compromise, being ready, as he said in a famous sentence, to deal with the devil himself in the interests of the Church. He was further persuaded by the fact that Mussolini had instructed his cohorts that they should be particularly respectful to the clergy and to their churches. Moreover, at this time most Italians regarded the Duce as a beneficent force for decency and law and order. And Pius XI was no democrat. 'With Mussolini,' the pope declared, 'much can be achieved.'

Mussolini for his part more than justified this confidence (though from time to time, when he did not get his way with the Church, he became threatening and truculent). He decreed that the clergy should be paid more. As for Catholic education – a cause especially dear to the pope – he decreed that every schoolroom should display a Crucifix. He added that the spiritual welfare of his soldiers should be cared for by Catholic army chaplains. He even condemned freemasons.

Soon Cardinal Pietro Gasparri had entered long, tedious, complicated and secret negotiations with the Italian State. Mussolini's deal was that the Vatican would relinquish its support for the Partito Popolare. Gasparri agreed. The dictator also relished the notion of the public approval of the supreme pontiff for his totalitarian regime. Soon, with the consent of the Vatican, Catholic leagues were marching alongside fascist supporters.

The result of these compromises was the Lateran agreements, signed between Italy and the papacy on 11 February 1929. By them the Vatican received 1,750 million Lire, enough to solve its financial worries. The concordat ratifying these agreements declared Catholicism the only State religion. Catholicism was to be taught in all State schools. Marriages conducted by the Church were accepted by the Italian State as valid. Clergy on criminal charges should be given special treatment. On the other hand, those priests and religious accused of apostasy or otherwise under the censure of the Church should be denied all civil rights. And the treaty solved the Roman question, which had dogged the papacy for sixty-two years. As Pius XI contentedly put it, he had 'given Italy back to God and God back to Italy.' One curious consequence was that Pius XI was now free to give daily audiences to privileged visitors, the first time a Roman pontiff had adopted the practice. Pius XI came to enjoy these audiences so much that he sometimes gave two in one day.

In December of that same year Pius XI published an encyclical, *Divini illius magistri*, on Christian education, which affirmed his belief that in this field there could be harmony between Church and State. Incidentally, this encyclical revealed him as a man of his time – one who deplored, for instance, co-education. At the same time, from his Church's point of view, he proclaimed a kind of pluralism, attacking the State's monopoly of schools.

Germany proved a much thornier problem than Italy. Overseen by the pope, concordats were signed with various German states to make the Church's position more stable. Now Eugenio Pacelli, longtime papal nuncio in Germany and since 1930 Cardinal Pietro Gasparri's successor as secretary of state to the pope, was instructed in 1933 to negotiate a concordat with the new regime of Adolf Hitler.

Almost all the German Catholic bishops had consistently opposed the Nazis. Their favoured politicians belonged to the *Zentrum*, the German Catholic party led by the cleric Monsignor Ludwig Kaas, which held out against Hitler's attempt to take omnipotent power until 1934. The pope thought otherwise. In his view Hitler, like himself, was a statesman praiseworthily and implacably opposed to Russian communism. The German bishops were persuaded to change their tune. And so, eventually, was Kaas's Catholic party.

Indeed, it was Kaas who in March 1933 went to Rome with Franz von Papen, the German vice-chancellor, to negotiate the concordat between the papacy and Hitler's Germany. Three months later the concordat was signed.

Pius moved more circumspectly with Spain and the rise to power of the dictator Francisco Franco, even though most

Italian Catholic leaders (as well as the German Catholic bishops) far preferred Franco to the Spanish republicans, whom they considered dangerously close to the communists. With the civil war, one of the most Catholic countries in Europe seemed to the Vatican to be threatened by unbelief. Not surprisingly, Pius XI himself publicly came out in favour of the Spanish fascists and against the Spanish republicans.

The paradox is that Pius XI's concordats sought to protect the freedom of the Church by alliances with regimes bent on suppressing freedom, regimes moreover (and particularly that of National Socialism in Germany) that were perfectly willing to break a concordat if they saw fit. Yet, as his condemnation of the newspaper *Action française* displayed, Pope Pius XI was no believer in or necessarily a supporter of political despotism.

Throughout his reign this stern pontiff was particularly warm towards France, with the clear intention of carrying on his predecessor's conciliatory policies. In 1922, the first year of his reign, the first person he beatified was Ste Thérèse of Lisieux. Three years later he proclaimed 1925 a Holy Year for the promotion of sanctity and in that year canonised Thérèse. She was, he declared, his 'star'. He set up her statue in the gardens of the Vatican. He proclaimed her protector of Mexico and Russia. And one of her relics was always by his bedside. Throughout the Maurras affair he commissioned the nuns of Lisieux continually to pray for the French Church.

He meant, of course, that they should pray that his own will prevailed, for this warmth did not imply weakness. During the Maurras affair French royalists and a good number of anti-republican bishops in France had bitterly accused the pope of not only democratic but also unpatriotic movements. Initially many of them had refused to go along with the papal condemnation. Conscious as always of his own authority, Pius XI cracked down on them, forcing the French bishops to sign a letter agreeing with his views, while lesser clergy and seminarians professing support for *Action française* were savagely disciplined. Cardinal Louis Billot suffered most. Imprudently he sent a letter commiserating with the editors of the newspaper. The pope summoned him to Rome and there peremptorily took back Billot's cardinal's hat.

Perhaps an inevitable, but unexpected, complement to this severity was the pope's ability to fly into a rage. He would bang his desk with his fists. Sometimes the technique worked, as, for example, when he was presiding at a meeting to consider the beatification of Brother Benaldo of the Christian Schools. Someone objected that Benaldo had been overly severe on pupils. The pope slammed his fist on the table, with the exclamation, 'If he hadn't been severe on the boys in his class, there would have been no more discipline, indeed no more studying.' At this everyone in the room gave in.

Often he would rise indignantly to his feet and shout at some visitor who had offended him or been summoned for a rebuke. Ally of totalitarian regimes, this was a totalitarian pope. Sometimes the pope realised that his rages had gone too far and the following day would profusely apologise, sending his unfortunate victim lavish presents. But he remained totalitarian. A young monsignor once asked. 'What, your holiness, are your wishes?' The pope retorted, 'Our predecessor Pius X preferred the word "commands" to "wishes".'

Pius XI would need all these reserves of steeliness in relation to the Nazi regime. After signing the concordat, almost immediately the German regime had broken some of its agreements with the papacy. Priests and layfolk were persecuted on invented charges. Catholic youths were seduced into semi-pagan organisations. Anti-Semitism and other forms of racial discrimination proliferated. In private Pius XI scandalised some less candid opponents of National Socialism by comparing the treatment of Christians in the Third Reich to the persecutions of the emperor Julian the Apostate. In public he condemned the Austrian episcopate in a statement which, read in every Austrian Catholic church after the German-Austrian *Anschluss* of 1938, fulsomely praised the Nazi regime.

He was for a long time less outspoken about Nazi anti-Semitism. The pope had remained silent when the National Socialists had passed their anti-Semitic laws of 1933 (though at that time Mussolini himself felt constrained to remonstrate with the German government about these measures). He had failed to condemn the racialist Nuremberg Laws of 1935, which forbade marriages between Aryans and Jews. Even when on the notorious *Kristallnacht* of 9 and 10 November 1938 Jewish synagogues throughout Germany had been destroyed by Nazi thugs, the Holy Father said nothing. And Pius XI never disowned the Vatican's concordat with Hitler, insisting, rightly or wrongly, that without it Catholic youth organisations could have been abolished and Catholic education brought to an end.

But in the end he did act, decisively, against the Nazi regime and its repeated violations of the concordat. Between 1933 and 1936, thirty-four notes of protest to the Reich government about these violations had been ignored. By the time of his most decisive move, the pope was seriously ill. His action was prompted by the German bishops, who at their annual conference in 1936 begged him for an encyclical setting out his views.

The sick pope was obliged to receive the German Church leaders (led by Cardinals Faulhaber and Bertram, along with Bishop Clemens August von Galen of Münster and Bishop von Preysing of Berlin) in his bed. Together, with Faulhaber the chief author, they drew up in German, the remarkable encyclical

Mit brennender Sorge (With Burning Anxiety). Lest the German authorities suppressed it, the encyclical was not sent by post but instead smuggled into Germany by private persons, to be read from every Catholic pulpit.

The encyclical stopped short of totally condemning National Socialism. But it was nonetheless remarkably intransigent. The idea of a German national Church, declared *Mit brennender Sorge*, was the denial of the Church of Christ. Such a Church was inevitably enslaved to earthly powers. Its teachings were counterfeit Christianity, a surrogate faith with nothing in common with the faith of the cross. 'We therefore say to the young, "Should anyone preach to you a gospel different from the one you received at the knees of a pious mother, from the lips of a Catholic father, from the teachings of one true to his God and his Church, let that person be anathema."'

Mit brennender Sorge condemned those who made 'race, nation and state' the supreme norm of all values, adding, 'The culmination of revelation in the gospel of Jesus Christ is final and binding for ever.' An infuriated Hitler ordered the seizure of all copies of the encyclical and in reprisal closed down the Catholic printing presses in his Reich. Nazi propagandists were ordered to vilify the pope. *Wille und Macht*, the periodical of the Reich youth leader Baldur von Schirach, sneered at 'the sickly wearer of the mitre'. Although the pope had not specifically mentioned the Jews in his encyclical, *Das Schwarze Korps* described him as the 'Chief Rabbi of all Christians'.

Soon the pope rose from his sickbed. When Hitler visited Rome, Pius XI withdrew to Castel Gandolfo, closing the Vatican museums (supposedly for repair work) to prevent Hitler's entourage from visiting them. He protested that a false cross, the swastika, had been displayed on a flag in Via della Conziliazione, which leads up to St Peter's Square. 'On the feast of the

Holy Cross,' he lamented, 'openly is displayed another cross, which is not the cross of Christ.'

Pius XI never doubted that National Socialism would perish. He would quote Psalm 68: 'Let God arise, and let his enemies be scattered.' Just as previous empires – that of Napoleon III, that of Bismarck – had foundered, so, the pope declared, Hitler's Reich would also collapse. And at last, in September 1938 he declared that anti-Semitism was utterly unacceptable, adding, 'spiritually we are all Semites.' It was to some Belgian pilgrims to the Vatican that he declared that Catholics were the spiritual heirs of the Jews.

In these circumstances this was an extraordinarily outspoken remark. Yet in the matter of ecumenicism Pius XI was less than eirenic. This intelligent, sensitive pope nonetheless failed to ascribe sufficient status to what he referred to as the 'schismatic' Eastern Orthodox Church for any of their distinguished leaders to accept his overtures. For him, submission to Rome was the *sine qua non* of reunion.

Pius XI totally dismissed the meetings of the burgeoning ecumenical movement among Protestants. In 1928 he declared that it was entirely wrong for Catholics to give their assemblies any support and that the Holy See would in no way take part in them – simply because Christian unity depended on the return of non-Catholics to Rome. 'There is but one way in which the unity of Christians can be fostered,' he declared, 'and that is by furthering the return to the one true Church of Christ of those who are separated from it: from that one true Church from which in the past they have fallen away.'

The same attitude stifled some extraordinary attempts by Cardinal Désiré Mercier, Archbishop of Malines, and the English Anglo-Catholic Lord Halifax to facilitate some reunion between Anglicans and Rome which would recognise the validity of the orders of Anglican priests. Over these negotiations the pope was not entirely ill-advised. Halifax by no means spoke for all Anglicans; but he was reasonably saddened to come away from his meeting with Pius XI in 1927 without any mention from the pope of the Malines conversations on unity, and was yet more put down when a papal decree soon forbade any more official or semi-official explorations of Anglican-Catholic reunion.

The pope also took upon himself to beatify and canonise a good number of Catholic martyrs of the English Reformation: 136 of them beatified in 1929, and John Fisher and Thomas More canonised in 1933 – two men who had lost their lives for refusing to accept King Henry VIII as the supreme authority in matters spiritual in England. These were not actions designed to mollify the Anglican communion.

To those who conceded that the pope should have a primacy of honour in the Church, though on the basis of equality between the different Churches, he replied that he had no intention of presiding 'over their kaleidoscopic conferences.' His view was perfectly clear. 'We do not know how any way is to be found to Church unity save through the one teaching authority' – namely the papacy. And his *Rerum Orientalium* was adamant that negotiations with Eastern Orthodox Churches should be conducted entirely on the pope's own terms.

In short, Pius XI was no less aware than his predecessor of the measure of his own authority. Asked once by a member of the curia whether he ought to consult its members more, the pope responded magnificently, 'We are the curia.' Pius XI believed the function of the curia to be to execute his own commands and to bring about the fulfilment of his own wishes. His 1925 encyclical *Quas Primas* declared that Christ was king over the whole of humanity – whether people recognised this or not – and Christ's representative was, of course, the pope himself.

Pius XI reigned as supreme pontiff for seventeen years. For fifteen he was in perfect health. In August 1936 he felt unwell, but soon recovered. In October he fainted and his head hit against a pillar. In December 1936 he fell seriously ill. He recovered, but his heart remained weakened, he was asthmatic and arterio-sclerosis had set in.

Yet these were the years of three of his most powerful encyclicals: *Divini Redemptoris* (condemning atheistic communism), *Mit brennender Sorge* and *Firmissima constantiam* (devoted to the problems of the Church in Mexico). His mind remained clear. Still able to bless the people each Easter from the outer loggia of St Peter's; still delighted at the building at Lisieux of a basilica in honour of Ste Thérèse and still able to jest, he faced his own mortality with a quip, asking Cardinal Antonio Bacci if he knew why so few people reached the age of ninety; Bacci was nonplussed, till the pope gave the answer, 'Because they die sooner.'

Two years passed before the end, the pope still giving audiences, meditating and walking in the Vatican gardens where he would pause by the statue of Ste Thérèse. But at last he was truly failing. On the first Sunday in February 1939 he was not strong enough to celebrate Mass. Recovering some of his strength, he received a group of Roman children who had won the diocesan cathechism competition. The pope blessed each one of them, and gave them all pictures of the supposed face of Jesus, reproduced from the Holy Shroud of Turin.

This was his last public act. Achille Ratti died just after half-past five on the morning of 10 February 1939, in his eighty-second year. As he lay dying, he would repeatedly touch the statue and relic of Ste Thérèse of Lisieux beside his bed. And this courageous old man who as a youth had been received into the third order of St Francis of Assisi, continually repeated on his death bed the words of St Francis: 'My God and my all.' He was buried in St Peter's, Rome, as he wished close by the tomb of Pope Pius X, his own effigy fittingly guarded by statues of St Ambrose of Milan and Ste Thérèse of Lisieux.

CHAPTER FIVE

Pius XII

Few anticipated the death of Pius XI. He forced his doctors to keep his terminal illness a secret. He longed to survive until the eleventh of the month, the tenth anniversary of the signing of the Lateran treaties. He longed to live a day longer, to receive in Rome the Italian bishops, whom he had summoned to a conclave. He begged his physicians to prolong his life. They failed to do so.

Of his successor, Pope John Paul II wrote in 1979,

> I shall never forget the deep impression which came over me when I first saw Pope Pius XII at close quarters. In this fortieth anniversary of the beginning of this important pontificate, we cannot forget the immense contribution made by Pius XII to the theological preparation for the Second Vatican Council, particularly by his teaching on the Church, by the new impetus which he gave to Biblical studies and by his profound attention to the problems of the contemporary world.

By contrast, in 1963 the German playwright Rolf Hochhuth assailed the memory of Pius XII with his play *Der Stellvertreter* (The Representative). Hochhuth alleged that, by failing to make any public protest against the Nazi extermination of Jews, Pope Pius XII was responsible for many Jewish deaths. Hochhuth might well be regarded as a man writing an exaggerated drama; but a year after the first staging of *Der Stellvertreter*, the Roman Catholic Cardinal Archbishop of Munich, Julius Doepfner, insisted from the pulpit that Pius XII should have protested with much greater zeal.

Others, notably Gitta Sereny, also took up the cudgels against the pope. Another polemicist, Paul Johnson, declared in his *History of Christianity* that 'Pius XII could hardly wait to send Hitler a friendly letter.' Paul Johnson, himself a Roman Catholic, added that eventually Pius XII told the college of cardinals that Nazism was satanic – an 'arrogant apostasy from Jesus Christ, the denial of his doctrine and his work of redemption, the cult of violence, the idolatry of race and blood, the overthrow of liberty and dignity.' But, Johnson adds devastatingly, 'it was then June 1945, the Germans had surrendered and Hitler was safely dead.'

Eugenio Maria Giuseppe Giovanni Pacelli, the subject of these denigrations, was born into a family of lawyers who had served the papacy for more than a century. Marcantonio Pacelli, his grandfather, was one of the founders of the Vatican newspaper *L'Osservatore Romano*. His uncle Ernesto headed the Banco di Roma. Francesco Pacelli, the future pope's elder brother, had represented Pius XI in the negotiations with Mussolini that resulted in the Lateran agreements.

As a student at the Liceo Visconti in Rome, Eugenio Pacelli excelled in languages, particularly French and German. At the Gregorian university and the Sapienza state university he shone in law (both civil and canon) and theology. On Easter Sunday 1899, the future pope was ordained priest. Soon he would be a member of the Roman curia.

His career flourished. It started in 1901 when he became a humble member of the papal secretariat of state. Between 1904 and 1916, when Cardinal Gasparri was codifying canon law, his chief assistant was Pacelli. As his career progressed he represented the Vatican in Austria and negotiated on its behalf with France.

In 1917 he achieved a new high when Pope Benedict XV consecrated Eugenio Pacelli Archbishop of Sardes and appointed him nuncio to the former Bavarian court in Munich. Pacelli was enjoined to convey to the German State the pope's abortive plan to bring about a European peace.

Presenting his credentials to King Ludwig of Bavaria on 28 May, Pacelli declared that a just and lasting peace could be based only on the firm basis of Christian law. 'Set as he is above human passion, in the clear realms of justice and love, the pope – protector, teacher and leader of men in their efforts to preserve and apply to the problems of humanity the precepts of natural law and Christian morality – strives for nothing else but to hasten the coming of the long-desired peace,' he said.

His, then, was a reasoned and high view of the role of the papacy. His subsequent actions as pope questioned whether or not he himself had lived up to them.

The next month he met the German emperor and urged on him the same message. Pacelli had a specific proposal, that Kaiser Wilhelm II stop the deportation of Belgian workmen to Germany. Wilhelm retorted that the deportation was perfectly legal, but promised to do something about it. He did nothing.

The short-lived communist republic which was set up in Bavaria at the end of the war brought the nuncio a threat of personal danger. At one point he returned to his residence to find it occupied by armed men who demanded that the archbishop hand over his carriage to them. Facing the insurgents alone, Pacelli managed to persuade them to go away empty-handed. (As he later told his doctor, again and again, even in his eightieth year he had nightmares connected with this event.) Diplomatically he had an equally difficult task: to negotiate a concordat with Bavaria, which was finally signed on 29 March 1924.

By this time the archbishop had been given the more important post of nuncio to the whole German nation. If negotiating a concordat with Catholic Bavaria had been difficult, to find some agreement with Protestant Prussia seemed impossible. Yet Pacelli was determined to establish some official *modus vivendi* between Church and State, some mutual understanding which would allow the Church what the archbishop later described as her 'complete independence to fulfil her divine calling.'

Eventually Otto von Braun, the socialist Prussian prime minister, was persuaded that a concordat was desirable, and managed to persuade his party likewise. The concordat with Prussia was finally ratified by the Prussian parliament on 13 August 1929, 243 members (including of course the Catholic centre party, led by Monsignor Ludwig Kaas) voting for it, 170 voting against.

By the terms of the concordat a new diocese was set up in Berlin, another in Aachen. But Otto von Braun deemed it prudent to omit any reference to Catholic schools in the document, reassuring Pacelli and the papacy by means of a letter annexed to the concordat that confessional schools and religious education were guaranteed by the Prussian constitution. Pacelli's personal secretary, Fr. Robert Leiber, conceded that the nuncio had achieved everything possible in the concordat.

Six months after it was signed Eugenio Pacelli was back in Rome as a member of the college of cardinals, and on 7 February the following year, on the death of Cardinal Gasparri, Pacelli replaced him as the pope's secretary of state. Here he was instrumental in concluding three more concordats, that with Baden in 1932, another with Austria in 1933 and one with Yugoslavia in 1935. Pacelli and Pope Pius XI worked hand in hand, condemning the Italian fascists in 1931 when they ignored the concordat with Italy and tried to stamp out the Catholic youth organisations, and attempting to cope with the Church's difficulties in 1932 in Mexico.

A year later the Nazis came to power in Germany. When the Reichstag passed the enabling act of 1933 by 441 votes to 94, allowing Adolf Hitler's government to pass laws without the consent of the German parliament, as we have seen Monsignor Ludwig Kaas's centre party voted for it, only the German social democrats opposing what amounted to the beginning of the Nazi dictatorship. And in that year, almost entirely under the guidance of Eugenio Pacelli, the Catholic Church decided to begin its most controversial act, negotiating with Hitler's government to bring about the fateful concordat with Nazi Germany.

As Pius XI explained in his forceful encyclical *Mit brennender Sorge*, the Church was ready to extend its peaceful and motherly hand to anyone who did not openly refuse it. The new German government wanted a concordat, and the leaders of the German Catholic Church supported this desire, as did many of the Catholic laity. Adolf Hitler wanted it, and was prepared to break his word whenever he thought it necessary. Soon state Catholic schools in Prussia and private Catholic schools in Austria were repressed; religious education in Bavarian Catholic schools was hampered; Sisters of Mercy were expelled from hospitals; Church charities in Austria were restricted; Church organisations had been dissolved, their endowments and property confiscated; the National-Socialist press increasingly put out anti-Catholic propaganda; and Catholic youth groups were closed down, as were some Catholic elementary schools.

As papal secretary of state, Pacelli was to make fifty-four written protests about these breaches of the concordat. The German government replied to a mere four of them. In spite of these diplomatic snubs, the Vatican under Pius XI did not cease to condemn German aggression. In his Christmas address of 1937, the pope lamented the 'terrifying and grievous persecution' in Nazi Germany. As we have also seen, the following year, when Germany's annexation of Austria was welcomed by the Cardinal Archbishop of Vienna, Pius XI summoned him to Rome and forced the archbishop to write a retraction.

Meanwhile Pacelli was undertaking missions on behalf of the Church to Buenos Aires, to Rio de Janeiro, to Lourdes, to his master's favoured Lisieux, to Paris and to the United States of America, as well as to South America. On his last such mission, to Budapest in 1938, he expressed his fears for the future of Europe. In Europe husband and wife distrusted each other, he judged, as did the different social classes, the people and the nations, which were indulging in a 'relentless race for rearmament'.

In France he was conspicuous for his condemnation, from pulpits at Lisieux and in Notre-Dame-de-Paris, of the racialism which was leading astray the 'noble' German nation. And all the time he was impressing men who would be influential when after the death of Pius XI a conclave would meet to determine his successor.

Cardinal Eugenio Pacelli was elected pope on the very first day of the Conclave of March 1939, receiving forty-eight out of fifty-three votes. His predecessor and mentor had made no secret that he wanted Pacelli to succeed him as supreme pontiff. As many said after the new election, Pius XI was still commanding, but now from Heaven. He had once indiscreetly said that if he had been able to take part in the conclave after his death, undoubtedly he would have voted for Pacelli.

Thirty-five of the cardinals assembled in Rome were Italian. Six came from North and South America. One came from Lebanon. Nearly all of them had met and grown to admire the sixty-three-year-old Pacelli. Pacelli told them that he foresaw immense ills about to afflict the world, and that the papacy was called to assuage them. On 2 March the balloting began, and shortly before half-past five in the afternoon white smoke announced that a pope had been elected. From the balcony of St Peter's Cardinal Camillo Caccia-Dominioni announced his name: Eugenio Pacelli. Then the new pope himself appeared, to bless the world.

'They've made a gondola out of the bark of St Peter,' acidly remarked the distinguished French historian and Academician Louis Duchesne, when Pius X brought his entourage of Venetians to Rome. But most popes behaved in this way, and on his election Pius XII brought a bevy of German prelates to the Vatican and staffed his personal household with German nuns.

His pontificate was to be judged by his attitude to the German nation where he had so signally served his predecessor. On 6 March he wrote 'to the illustrious Herr Adolf Hitler, Führer and Chancellor of the German nation', recalling with immense pleasure his many years in Germany as apostolic nuncio, 'when we did all in our power to establish harmonious relations between Church and State.' Now, the new pope added, he had been given even greater opportunities to work towards the same goal.

Meanwhile the Third Reich had annexed Bosnia and Moravia. In London the Archbishop of Canterbury, Cosmo Gordon Lang, made an impassioned appeal in the House of Lords for the world's Christian communities to unite in condemning such aggression and in defending justice and freedom. Remarkably, the Anglican primate suggested that much depended on whether His Holiness the Pope would be willing to give his leadership. Lang suggested that it might be that the pope felt his recent election had occurred precisely for this hour, at a time when Christendom was called upon to condemn a new exaltation of the State over the human personality and the use of force to decide international questions. The archbishop insisted that if the pope would offer such leadership, Anglicans, Protestants and Orthodox Christians would surely simultaneously support him.

Faithful to his revulsion from ecumenical relations that might compromise his own supreme position, the pope refused to respond.

Like his mentor Pius XI, Pope Pius XII never disowned the Vatican's concordat with Hitler, insisting, rightly or wrongly, that without it Catholic youth organisations could have been abolished and Catholic education brought to an end. When the Second World War was over, he continued to defend the concordat with Nazi Germany. In 1945 he told the Catholic cardinals that in the years succeeding 1933, the concordat brought advantages to the Church in Germany, or at least prevented greater evils than if no concordat had been agreed. 'Though often violated, it gave Catholics a legal ground of defence, a platform from which to resist as long as possible the tide of persecution.' In this spirit he signed three more concordats with totalitarian regimes: Portugal, Spain and the Dominican Republic.

In the intervening years the pope had striven to divide the Axis powers. He tried in vain to persuade Mussolini not to side with Hitler. He was amongst those who succeeded in persuading Spain to stay neutral. It seemed to him that an international conference, not war, would best settle the differences of the great powers, and he broadcast in 1939 a moving appeal for peace.

Fortunately, too, the papal diplomats had managed to establish good relations with the Americans, and President Franklin D. Roosevelt dispatched a special envoy to the Vatican. Twice Roosevelt wrote to Mussolini in an attempt to keep him out of the war. When Italy's entry into the war threatened the city of Rome itself, the pope made a special appeal to the Americans and their allies to spare the city.

In the August that preceded the outbreak of the Second World War, as Hitler prepared to invade Poland, the pope made another appeal for a truce, to enable an international conference to deal with the matter. 'Nothing is lost with peace,' he said, 'but everything may be lost by war.' But Hitler was determined to invade Poland, whatever the pope's views. When war broke out, Pius XII, the first pope to rule a sovereign state since 1846, declared his realm neutral, though he continued to appeal for Poland, a land as his first encyclical put it, 'imperishably crowned in the pages of history by her long record of loyalty to the Church and for her services to Christian civilization.'

Poland, in particular its Catholics and its Catholic Church, was especially dear to the pope's heart. Hitler violated the autonomy of that Church. He declared that every Polish province on the borders of Germany was annexed to the Third Reich. These provinces incorporated parts of important Polish dioceses of Gniezno, Warsaw, Czestochowa, Wladislava and

Lodz as well as the whole of the diocese of Poznan. Hitler insisted on a veto on any new episcopal appointment. As a result, few were made.

But still the pope remained silent on the Nazis' behaviour: their profaning of churches (many of which had been closed down); their seizing of Church property; their imprisonment of nuns; and their murder of thousands, including not only Jews and members of the Polish intelligentsia but also Catholic priests, while other clergy were sent along with Jews to concentration camps.

Bishop Hilary Breitenger asked whether the pope had forgotten the Poles. 'Why,' he said, 'does the pope remain silent?' Archbishop Adam Stephen Sapieha of Krakow begged for a word of reproof from the pope for the way Germany was harassing the Polish Church. None came. Exiled in London, Bishop Radonski of Wladislava said bluntly, 'a man who does not speak, consents.'

We now know that Pius XII felt that, to condemn Nazi atrocities in Poland, he would also need to condemn those of the Soviets, which would offend the allies, with whom the USSR had eventually sided. He also, as ever, feared reprisals should he speak out. Only in June 1943 did Pius XII finally consent openly to condemn the sufferings inflicted on Poland. There were no Nazi reprisals.

Similarly, when Archbishop Stepinac of Zagreb protested against the German persecution of Jews in Croatia, the persecution ceased. If the murder of six million Jews, half of them brought from other parts of Europe than Poland, remains a horrific memory, it is easy to forget the killing of some half-a-million Croatians whose Orthodox faith ill-fitted with the Catholicism of their masters. Yet Pius XII remained silent about this too.

In 1918 Croatia had become part of the kingdom of the Croats, Serbs and Slovenes, known as Yugoslavia from 1929. It was an unstable union, Serbs and Croats particularly disliking each other. The former had frequently humiliated the latter. Moreover, in religion the Croats were Orthodox, whereas the Serbs were passionately Catholic. Serbs looked to the east; Croats to the west, and especially to their spiritual leaders, the popes. Pope Leo X had described Croatia as an 'outpost of Christianity' in an alien land.

During the Second World War this outpost of Catholic Christianity was surrounded on all sides by the axis powers, and on 10 April 1941 German troops entered Zagreb. The Nazis set up a state which they called Greater Croatia, under a puppet ruler, Ante Pavelic. Pavelic was an ally of Benito Mussolini and had long been a leading fascist in the Balkans. Unlike Mussolini and most Italians, he was also viciously anti-Semitic. Seeking to establish a 'pure' Catholic republic, his Croatian régime eventually massacred some 100 thousand Serbs and fifty-five thousand Jews. Initially, however, his régime 'persuaded' some two-and-a-quarter thousand Serbs who lived in Croatia to convert from Orthodoxy to Catholicism.

By coincidence, 1941 was the thirteenth centenary of the conversion of Croatia to Catholicism. Pius XII granted the country a special Jubilee – a holy year in which special indulgences were granted to faithful Catholics, above all to those who made a pilgrimage to Rome. Few had the means to visit Rome, but other indulgences, which included forgiveness of sins and remittance of punishment in the next world, were granted to those who solemnly renewed their baptismal vows or indulged in other spiritual exercises.

But much of Pavelic's programme was anathema to the Catholic leaders in Croatia. The archbishops and bishops, though entirely in favour of any submission by the Orthodox to Catholicism, had little faith in forced conversions, and they decisively informed the government of their views. Archbishop Aloysius Stepinac of Zagreb consistently disapproved of these mass conversions. 'Faith,' he wrote, 'is a matter of free conscience, and therefore dishonest motives must be excluded from any decision to embrace it.' And in this he and his fellow prelates were supported by the Holy See.

Croatia is close to Italy, and Pius XII was well aware of what was going on in that country, both during and after the Second World War. In spite of Pavelic's brutality to non-Catholics, the Vatican State established *de facto* diplomatic relations with Croatia. The pope received Pavelic in the Vatican City, praising him as a sincere Catholic yet never once referring to the barbarity of his régime towards the Orthodox and the Jews. As the war drew to its close, on 2 June 1945 Pius XII finally brought himself to condemn the murder of priests (of his own flock), the vengeful massacre of citizens without trial and the deportation of civilians.

Thus Pius XII's policy of neutrality in the run-up to and during the Second World War, a policy which few today think justifies his refusal to condemn Germany, did not prevent him condemning acts of aggression by communists, and particularly by communist Russia. When the Russian army invaded Poland in 1939, the pope was swift to attack the 'threatening and sinister shadow of the enemies of God'. When Germany invaded a Russia that was in religion Orthodox and in theory atheistic, he was inwardly pleased.

Again, he was following in the footsteps of Pius XI. 'Communism is intrinsically evil,' Pius XI's encyclical *Divini Redemptoris* had declared, 'and so no one who desires to save from extinction Christian civilization should give it the remotest assistance in any of its enterprises.' His successor took the same line.

This inborn stance was to have stern consequences not only for the Church's social gospel but also for its outreach amongst the urban proletariat. The pope's fear of communism scotched a French initiative to reach out to working men and women through the ministry of 'worker-priests'. Cardinal Emmanuel Suhard, Archbishop of Paris, ardently supported the worker-priest movement, but soon some of these worker-priests were openly supporting communist trades unions. The cardinal was sanguine to expect that Pius XII would support such a development, and when Suhard died in 1949 the pope became increasingly hostile to the idea of a worker-priest movement: 1953 saw the end of the bold, if dangerous initiative.

Already in 1942, when the so-called 'final solution' to the 'Jewish problem' was put into effect by the Nazi régime, six diplomats from the neutral and allied nations had begged the pope to condemn the atrocities and abandon his policy of silence. Pius XII refused to heed them. He procrastinated. Although he repeatedly condemned war crimes, he never named the Nazis in his attacks.

Pius XII learned from his own sources of the mass extermination of Jews in Germany, Poland and the Ukraine in May 1942. Detailed information came particularly from chaplains travelling through Poland on the hospital trains of the Sovereign Order of Malta. As one wrote, 'in our periodical journeys by Auschwitz, only a few yards separated us from that infamous enclosure. At night we could see the searchlights from the watch-towers slowly turning in a pointless quest for impossible escapers, while the acrid smell from the crematoria reached us in nauseating whiffs.'

In September 1942 the personal representative in Rome of

President F. D. Roosevelt delivered a request from the president to condemn the atrocities of those parts of Europe occupied by Germany. The pope, he strongly urged, should denounce the inhuman treatment of refugees, and above all of the Jews. In October a message from Roosevelt specifically referred to the German massacre of Jews in Russia, describing them as surpassing everything known since the most brutal and bestial epochs of mankind.

Perhaps because of such pressure, the pope's Christmas message that year did go so far as to condemn the way hundreds of thousands of innocent people, without any fault of their own, were being marked out for death or doomed to slow extinction, sometimes merely because of their nationality or race.

He never again referred to the mass exterminations. It seemed to him that he had done enough. As he told the Bishop of Berlin the following year, 'In our Christmas message we said a word about what is being perpetrated at present against non-Aryans in areas controlled by the Germans.' This word, the pope conceded, was summed up in a very short passage; but he insisted that it was perfectly understood. He then went on to reveal, almost unconsciously, that his primary concern had been and was the fate not so much of practising Jews but of Jews who had converted to Christianity. 'It hardly needs saying,' the pope continued, 'that now that they are being annihilated, our love and pastoral care for non-Aryan or semi-Aryan Catholics who are, like others, sons of the Church, ought to be all the greater.'

All this information and these prevarications scotch the arguments that Pius XII did not know what was happening to the Jews and to the other ethnic minorities threatened by Hitler. One of those who defended him was Robert Leiber, a Jesuit who served as the pope's personal secretary from 1924 until Pacelli's death. Twenty days after the end of the Second World War Pius

XII himself had tried to put the matter straight, by claiming in his address to the assembled Catholic cardinals that he had never ceased to oppose the ruthless Nazi doctrines which had resulted in using the most advanced scientific methods to torture and suppress often innocent people. His claim was false.

As the Church historian Paul Johnson observed, Pius XII had a lifelong affection for all things German.

> He had lived there for many years, and some of his very few close friends, as well as his household servants, were German. He could not, or would not, or at all events did not, distinguish between the Nazi regime and the German people. He viewed with dread the prospect of a Europe in which the German state was shattered, and the German people – as he saw it – powerless to uphold Christian civilization.

Pius XII also feared the possibility that if Germany collapsed, Soviet Russia would take over the resulting political vacuum in Europe.

Indeed, the pope was desperate to preserve any links with Hitler's Germany. When Cardinal Archbishop Adolf Bertram of Wroclaw sent a birthday greeting to Hitler, Bishop Count Konrad von Presysing of Berlin decided to resign from the Bishops' Conference in protest. Pius XII persuaded him not to, for the sake of unity. And he wrote to Bertram, 'For us it is an imperious duty of conscience not to miss any opportunity which might ensure an acceptable peace between Church and State,' adding that even so he did not want peace at any price.

When the Nazis put into practice a programme of euthanasia, killing the incurably sick and also the aged, the German bishops appealed to Rome to condemn this. The Bishop of Münster,

Clemens August von Galen, was outspoken in condemnation, preaching brilliantly by suggesting that the authorities might soon consider killing wounded soldiers who had returned from the front and who were no longer useful for military or civil service. Von Galen specified clinics where Germans were already being put to death. No one, he insisted, was immune to this inhuman practice. 'Any committee can put someone on the list of "unproductives", having judged that person to have become "unworthy of human life".'

Von Galen had already attacked violations of the concordat, calling upon the authority of the papacy. All these violations were known to everyone, he pronounced, adding, 'The pope knows it too; should I then remain silent?' Once again the outspoken Bishop of Münster refused to keep silence. The euthanasia programme was halted. The question has to be faced: would the murder of Jews have been similarly halted had the pope not remained silent?

When the war was over, some sprang to the pope's defence. At the Nuremberg trials Albrecht von Kessel, a member of the Germans' wartime embassy at the Vatican, declared that the pope lodged no protest because he justifiably thought that if he did so Hitler would go crazy and the Jews would be killed even more speedily. More, added von Kessel, Hitler would probably have instructed the SS to storm the Vatican and lay hands on the pope himself.

Yet these scruples lie uneasily alongside the Vatican's protests to Nazi Germany over the persecution, imprisonment and even murder of Catholic bishops and priests. And fears for the pope's safety clash with Pius XII's own statement that if necessary he would submit willingly to incarceration in a concentration camp.

Pius XII did exert himself on behalf of the seven thousand or so Jews who lived in Rome. In September 1943 the SS ordered this community to hand over within twenty-four hours fifty kilos of gold. When the deadline came, the community had been able to gather together only thirty-five kilos. Pope Pius XII made up the shortfall. And when he learned from Ernst von Weizsäcker, German ambassador to the Vatican, that the SS had begun rounding up the Jews of Rome, he cooperated with the ambassador to prevent their deaths. Von Weizsäcker's telegram to Berlin can be used to vilify the pope but it might also have helped to save the Jews of the Vatican State from further persecution:

> Though under pressure from all sides, the pope has refused to be drawn into any open censure of the deportation of Jews from Rome. In this delicate matter, he has done everything possible not to strain relations with the government of Germany or with German circles in Rome. Since there is probably no reason to expect any more German actions against the Jews of Rome, we can consider that the problem so disturbing to German-Vatican relations no longer exists.

Such prevarications, subterfuges to save Jews and outright collaboration with the anti-Semitic policies of Adolf Hitler characterised Catholic action elsewhere in Europe. In Slovakia the head of state was a Catholic priest who faithfully carried out the Nazi racial policy, even though the Vatican *chargé d'affaires* strongly objected.

Yet there were exceptions. In Bulgaria Monsignor Angelo Giuseppe Roncalli (the future Pope John XXIII) intervened with King Boris to stop the deportation of Jews. In Holland the Bishop of Liège passed off the city's rabbi as his personal secretary. France was particularly callous in its treatment of its

Jews, deporting 150 thousand, but some Catholic priests and bishops (notably the Bishops of Lyons, Montauban and Toulouse) protested energetically. Archbishop Saliège of Toulouse declared, 'The Jews are our brethren.'

The Holy Father neither followed their lead nor gave them one. 'After many tears and many prayers,' so the pope is reported to have said to a military chaplain who told him of what was happening in the concentration camps, 'I judged that any protest of mine would not only fail to help any person but would also create even more fury against the Jews, multiplying acts of cruelty.' His under-secretary of state, later crowned as Pope Paul VI, never ceased to defend his former master on these lines. During the furore over Rudolf Hochhuth's *Der Stellvertreter*, Giovanni Battista Montini, then a cardinal, wrote to *The Tablet* that any open intervention by Pius XII would not only have been futile but also harmful, adding 'that is the long and short of the matter.'

Other considerations also influenced the pope's decisions. He enormously feared the extension of the war into Italy, a development that would threaten the Vatican State itself.

When the war was over much of the post-war world seemed hostile to Rome. Communist Romania got rid of its twelve Catholic archbishops and bishops, either by deporting or imprisoning them. Hungary imprisoned and tortured Cardinal Mindszenty. The Czechs, likewise under communist rule, dismissed thirteen bishops. Not surprisingly, Pius XII continued unreservedly to condemn communism, declaring that it placed the future of the world in the gravest peril. In 1947 he pronounced that those who supported godless forces or incited the masses to revolt were traitors.

By now numerous Catholics, especially in Italy, had joined communist parties. In 1947 the pope persuaded Alcide De

Gasperi, leader of the Christian Democrat party, to exclude communists from the Italian government. He even tried, in vain, to persuade De Gasperi to ban the communists altogether. Two years later the pope publicly censured Italian Catholics who still supported communism. At the same time, in an encyclical of that year, he acknowledged that there always remained the possibility of tyranny over workers from private capital as well as from the power of an overmighty, totalitarian state.

Other parts of the Marxist world seemed determined to humiliate the Vatican. At the end of the Second World War, in November 1945, Greater Croatia became one of the constituent republics of the Yugoslav Republic, ruled by the soldier, partisan and communist politician Marshal Tito. Tito had led the guerrillas who resisted the German invasion of 1941. His provisional government of 1943 had won recognition from the allies. Although the Russians effectively brought him to power in 1945, he managed to preserve a policy of non-alignment between the United States of America and the USSR. He also decided to prosecute Archbishop Stepinac for collaborating during the war with the Germans.

There is evidence that Tito had little desire to proceed with this prosecution and initially wished the Vatican simply to recall the archbishop to Rome. Pius XII refused and instead gave Stepinac a cardinal's hat. Eventually, in December 1963, the Holy See and Yugoslavia broke off relations. Stepinac was tried, imprisoned and then (on account of his failing health) released to spend the rest of his life under house arrest.

But politics, even in those desperate times, never stopped this pope from spiritual meditation. In the tormented year of 1943 Pius XII published two encyclicals. The first, *Mystici Corporis*, issued on 29 June, was devoted to the nature of the Church, defining it quite narrowly as the Roman Catholic Church and also mystically as involving the union of all Catholics with Christ.

The second, surprisingly radical encyclical of these wartime years, *Divino afflante Spiritu*, was issued on 30 September and dealt with Biblical studies. Here the pope sanctioned a new departure in Catholic Biblical studies by aligning himself with those theologians who wanted to follow lines of thinking already opened up by some Protestants. His encyclical distinguished between the different literary forms of scripture – thereby allowing for the notion that not all Biblical truth is expressed in the same way. In this encyclical Pius XII affirmed the rights of scholarship in Biblical interpretation and analysis, implicitly repudiating the view expressed by Leo XIII in 1893 that every statement of Holy Scripture was free from error.

Startlingly, then, the pope had reversed his predecessor's attitude to Biblical scholarship (though he later changed his mind). The attack on Modernists had no appeal for him, and he turned decisively against those who would anathematize scholars who wished to use every modern means of scholarship to study Holy Scripture. One major result was the *Jerusalem Bible*, which ranks alongside any work of late-nineteenth and twentieth-century Biblical scholarship, finally renouncing papal distrust of those savants (even German Protestants) who had fearlessly used every resource available to them in studying the sacred text.

He was less radical on the question of artificial contraception. In his encyclical *Casti connubii* Pope Pius XI had condemned it. His precept, said Pius XII, is as valid today as when he issued it – 'the expression of a law that is both natural and divine.' In 1968 Pope Paul VI's encyclical *Humanae Vitae* reaffirmed this teaching.

In between the issue of the first two of these encyclicals, *Mystici corporis* and *Divino afflante Spiritu*, the war had reached

Rome. On 19 July allied bombers attacked the marshalling yards and the main railway station of the city. As well as killing five hundred persons they also severely damaged the basilica of San Lorenzo. The pope left the Vatican to kneel there and to do what he could to comfort the people. He also grew less sanguine about the goodwill of President Roosevelt. Within a week Mussolini fell from power. The allies announced an armistice with Italy, but a day later, on 9 September 1943, the Germans occupied Rome.

Pius XII deemed 1950 a Holy Year and inaugurated it on Christmas Eve 1949. The Holy Year gave him the opportunity to proclaim as Catholic dogma the bodily Assumption of the Blessed Virgin Mary – something, of course, many Christians had believed for centuries. But the proclamation was in one important sense revolutionary. For the first time a pope was invoking his infallibility, as defined by the Vatican Council of 1870.

In his personal piety Pius XII was devoted to Mary, the mother of Jesus. But even now the pope did not strictly act alone; pressure to affirm the dogma had come from no fewer than eight million petitions from the Catholic faithful.

During the same year Pius XII also issued another, stunningly reactionary encyclical, *Humani generis.* Curiously enough, in his later years the pope seems to have repented of the generosity shown towards Biblical scholarship in *Divino afflante Spiritu*, and *Humani generis*, issued on 12 August 1950, retracted many of the concessions he had previously made to honest scholarship.

His concern was that too much emphasis on Biblical studies and the authority of the Bible could detract from the supremacy of papal authority. The pope, his new encyclical announced, was the 'living teacher', whose role was to illustrate and develop truths contained only obscurely and by implication in the storehouse of faith. Just such a 'truth' was the dogma of the bodily Assumption of the Virgin Mary.

Yet alongside this repeated concern for the supremacy of his office as vicar of Christ came a softening of his attitude to other Churches. When the World Council of Churches was set up in 1948, Pius XII formally recognised the ecumenical movement. He now blessed those of his own flock who entered into discussions with other Churches.

This pope reigned for nineteen years, seven months and seven days. In the last month of his life he gave seventeen addresses, and planned to give another three. He put it about that he had been given visions of Jesus, his first three in autumn 1950. Like St Francis of Assisi, he claimed an affinity with birds, and took to issuing photographs of himself with a budgerigar perched on his finger. He also attempted to prolong his own earthly life with hormone injections (derived from lambs' tissues) given by his friend the Swiss physician Paul Neihans.

The pope became seriously ill in 1954, but recovered, to live for another four years. Emaciated even when he became pope, emaciated even more during the war, when he cut down his food and refused to have his apartments heated in winter (thus reducing his six-foot frame to less than nine stones), his still gaunt physical appearance gave little evidence of his dire medical condition.

He also seems to have been possessed with an unearthly ambition. In 1954 Pius XII had declared that his predecessor, Pope Pius X, was a saint. He suggested that Pope Pius IX could also be sanctified. Above all he supposed that he himself might, after his death, be also officially canonised.

Once again he began releasing reports that he had received heavenly visions. Jesus himself was said to have appeared at the bedside of the ailing pontiff. His divine influence, it was alleged, was bringing many to the Catholic faith. A Roman tram-driver was produced, claiming that as a Protestant he had planned to knife the pope but that he was now a faithful Catholic, because the Blessed Virgin Mary had personally appeared to convert him.

The pope's last public appearance was on 6 October 1958, and three days later, in Castel Gandolfo, Pius XII was dead. One of his successors, Pope Paul VI, introduced the cause of canonisation for Pius XII, but he has yet to be beatified.

Canonisation usually requires evidence of something miraculous with a papal corpse, usually its immunity to decomposition (hence the exhumation of Pius X). The pope was therefore embalmed, but the method employed did not work. Even before his lying-in-state was over, his body began to decompose, and several of the guards standing ceremonial attention round the catafalque fainted. One of the first acts of his successor was to ban the embalming of the bodies of dead popes.

The following year Cardinal Domenico Tardini, a close friend of the deceased pope, gave a lecture commemorating the life of Pius XII. 'By natural temperament,' Tardini said, 'Pius was meek, indeed timid. His temper was not that of a fighter, unlike that of his great predecessor Pius XI, who visibly rejoiced in a contest.' Yet, Tardini added, Pope Pius XII was continually forced to fight.

Did he fight hard enough against Adolf Hitler? 'We cannot brand him with infamy, even if it does not absolve him from undoubted responsibility,' wrote the judicious Carlo Falconi in his assiduously researched study *The Silence of Pius XII*. Falconi generously added, 'In any case, a severe judgement on his silence does not exclude an open-minded and unconditional recognition of all that he did to prevent the outbreak of war, to discourage its spreading, and to alleviate the sufferings of its victims.' He longed for peace, and in 1943 rightly judged that Roosevelt and Churchill, insisting on the unconditional surrender of the Germans, had only prolonged the war. He went so far as to let Roosevelt know of his regret and disagreement.

Yet, Carlo Falconi continued, 'To sum up: Pius XII never formally condemned the outbreak of war, its development, nor all that it finally involved. Indeed he systematically avoided pronouncements about who was responsible for the war. His preaching, even when aimed at a wider audience than Catholics, was always confined to upholding the Church's preference for peace.'

CHAPTER SIX

John XXIII

'It is rare to achieve greatness in old age,' observed the historian J. H. Plumb, 'but that is exactly what Pope John XXIII achieved.'

From Pius XII he inherited a Church that, save in the matter of worship and Biblical scholarship, seemed to be stagnating. An iron curtain divided the communist world from the capitalist west, and the Catholic Church had not attempted to breach it. The worker–priest movement in France was distrusted. Numerous attempts to summon a Second Vatican Council in order to continue and extend the work of the abortive one of 1870 had come to nothing. And politically the Church remained deeply conservative. The arthritis which Pius XII suffered in his later years seemed also to have extended to the Church he had controlled.

In electing as pope Angelo Giuseppe Roncalli, the genial but aged Patriarch of Venice, the conclave of 1958 seemed to have made a conservative choice. He would reign for a mere four-and-a-half years. Yet he would surprise those who elected him with the words, 'We have to shake off the dust that has been accumulating on the throne of St Peter since the time of Constantine.'

Fifty-two cardinals arrived in Rome for the election, most of them Europeans, with fourteen from North and South America. India, China and Australia provided one each. From the desperate lands dominated by communism arrived one formidable man: Cardinal Wyszynski, the primate of Poland.

Eleven ballots took place before the new pope was elected. The man who eventually was chosen was aged, but he was strangely radical. As Patriarch of Venice Angelo Roncalli had championed modern art, had even been willing to welcome into his palace local communists, as well as being affable to socialists. His bulky figure, with its massive Roman nose and elephantine ears, appeared on the balcony of St Peter's just after a quarter past six in the evening, to give the traditional papal benediction, *Urbi et Orbi*.

On his election he said that he wished to follow Jesus as a good shepherd, adding that no other gift for a supreme pontiff could match that. So, following the demands of his master, two months after his election, on Christmas Day he could be found in Rome's Regina Coeli gaol, comforting the prisoners. As a pastoral Bishop of Rome he began to visit every one of the parishes under his episcopal control.

This was a delightfully honest man, happy for all his years serving the Catholic Church, sometimes in difficult realms. He had numerous relatives, not all of them belonging to the upper orders of Italian society. This was a pope whose family had often found it hard to feed every little mouth in the household. He took the name John (long derided because it had been claimed by an anti-pope) because, he said, that was the name of his father and the dedication of the church, San Giovanni, in which he had been baptised. And this humble pope was also a man who had successfully trodden the political and diplomatic stage of the Vatican, without ever succumbing to the lures of either arrogance or ambition, though at times sorely tempted by them.

Roncalli had been born in November 1881 in the northern Italian village of Sotto il Monte. Although his family were tenant-farmers, they were nevertheless proud of their escutcheon – a tower on a field of white and red bars – which decorated their house in the village, and when Angelo became a bishop he was equally proud to assume it as his coat of arms.

Angelo's parents had thirteen children, though two of them died young. Ten cousins also shared their farmhouse, so it seemed fitting in 1891 for the whole extended family to move to another, larger house with eighteen rooms. Traditional Italian piety pervaded the home and the rosary was recited each evening. Soon it became clear that Angelo, the most intelligent of the children, should train for the priesthood, and in preparation the parish priest began to teach him Latin. Two terms at a nearby diocesan seminary led to a place at the seminary of Bergamo, secured for him by a brother of his father's landlord, who was a canon of the cathedral there. He was tonsured in June 1895.

The diary which he began to keep from then on (on the instructions of his superiors) reveals an increasing gap between the young seminarian and his country family. He hated his holidays, when he was obliged to leave the seminary and live at home. They thought him a cut above their station and arrogant. He deplored their constant preoccupation with the daily grind. But he knew that pride, self-esteem, even arrogance, were his chief temptations.

Even in these youthful days, Angelo learned to keep his innermost thoughts to himself, later attributing this trait to the influence of his spiritual director at the Bergamo seminary, Fr. Francesco Pitocci, who also told him that austerity as a young man, linked to later experience, is the finest way of discovering the exact amalgam of truth, justice and charity. This guardedness, concealed by his personal warmth and love of jesting, helps to explain the surprise generated by Angelo Roncalli's radical transformation of the papacy. Outwardly he conformed; inwardly, as his journal reveals, he was his own man.

At the age of nineteen he left Bergamo for the pontifical seminary which had been founded in Rome by a canon of Bergamo cathedral on behalf of future priests from his own region. Angelo was present at the consecration of Pope Pius X, a man like himself born in the lower orders. And three years later the young man was ordained priest. Over the tomb of St Peter the day afterwards, he said his first Mass. On the feast of the Assumption of the Blessed Virgin Mary, Angelo Roncalli was back home in Sotto il Monte, to celebrate his first Mass before his assembled family. And when the new Bishop of Bergamo, Count Radini-Tedeschi, was consecrated in 1905, Angelo took the first step up the ladder of ecclesiastical preferment when the bishop invited him to become his secretary.

Radini-Tedeschi strongly believed that the Church should involve itself in the social problems of the day. This work was hampered by the ban on voting in elections at that time imposed on Italian Catholics. Only 20 per cent of the electorate of Bergamo disobeyed the ban and voted in the 1890 election. But before he was consecrated bishop, Radini-Tedeschi had attempted to circumvent this ban by fostering groups of Catholic layfolk who would influence workers on behalf of the Church and its social views. By the end of the century, when he was Bishop of Bergamo, some two hundred such groups, with over forty thousand members, had been set up in his diocese. When in 1909 he made a donation to a fund for local strikers, some members of the Roman curia were scandalised, but the bishop survived the scandal.

Along with his bishop, Roncalli was able to travel far, visiting France and Germany, Austria and Palestine. He remained with Radini-Tedeschi until the bishop died of cancer in 1914, not yet sixty years old. As an act of piety, Angelo then wrote a biography of his friend and mentor, *Monsignor Giacomo Maria Radini-Tedeschi*. His patron was rash and sometimes obstinate, Roncalli judged, but he was also transcendentally pure in spirit and open in heart.

Worldliness did not attract Roncalli. His compulsory military service took place in 1915 in the Bergamo army hospital, where he worked as a sergeant and grew a moustache. He found the atmosphere ugly, even, as he put it, loathsome – the soldiers were offensively blasphemous and some of them vulgar in behaviour and language.

Solace came from the Church. The late bishop's secretary continued to lecture in Church history at the Bergamo seminary. His approach was cautious, as he well knew that the anti-Modernist camp in the Church was on the rampage. Roncalli took heed of Radini-Tedeschi's advice: boldness consists of being prudent. Even so, he stood out against the extreme opponents of Modernism, writing against them in the diocesan magazine. When he became pope, he at last had access to his personal file in the curia. He read there the words, 'suspected of Modernism'.

Wisely, he confined most of his academic work to history, editing the papers of St Charles Borromeo, which were housed in the Ambrosian Library at Milan (whose librarian was Achille Ratti). Roncalli's edition appeared in five volumes, the last published when he was pope. He had also taken the trouble to send a copy of his life of Bishop Radini-Tedeschi to the bishop's old friend, who was now Pope Benedict XV. Benedict summoned him to Rome, to oversee, as president of the Italian central council for papal missions, the fund-raising activities for the Church's missionary work.

At last he had gained some recognition from the leaders of Catholicism. Roncalli was in the public eye. And a year later his friend the librarian of the Ambrosian Library was consecrated Pope Pius XI.

In 1924 Angelo Giuseppe Roncalli was made professor of patrology at the Lateran College. Here his reputation as a Modernist worked against him, and after only two terms in the post he was dismissed. The following year he was exiled, although with a new status. Remembering how he himself had been excluded from several important meetings when he was a 'mere' apostolic visitor to the Church in Poland in 1918, Pope Pius XI took care to give Roncalli sufficient status before sending him as his representative, or apostolic visitor, to Bulgaria. Angelo Roncalli was consecrated titular Archbishop of Areopolis. He stayed there for ten years.

There he had little to do. His flock consisted of some fifty thousand Catholics, many of them illiterate and poor, while the bulk of the population was Muslim. Angelo wished to establish a seminary, but the curia blocked the idea. He struck up a rapport with King Boris of Bulgaria, but feared that nothing would come of this since the apostolic visitor had been given no real power by the Vatican. His life, he wrote in his diary, was monotonous, that of a total hermit. Even King Boris snubbed him, assuring Roncalli that he would marry the daughter of King Victor Emmanuel III of Italy according to Catholic rites and then remarry her in the Orthodox Church.

Roncalli had incorporated in his episcopal coat of arms the words *Obedientia et pax* (Obedience and peace), and this spirit sustained him throughout what were in many ways tiresome, frustrating years. His sole reprieve was travel, to Turkey and Greece, to Romania and Poland, to Germany and Czechoslovakia.

Then at the age of fifty-four he was moved to Istanbul. Life improved. Here were some ten thousand Catholics. Here were Greeks, of the Orthodox faith. Here lived Turks, passionately Muslim when not, with equal passion, secularist. Angelo Roncalli took an interest in the Orthodox, devotedly visiting their monasteries and shrines. He also decided that the best way to deal with the Turks was to form unofficial friendships with members of the government. When Pius XI died in 1939 Angelo had so much charmed members of other communions and faiths that a service of commemoration arranged by Roncalli in Istanbul's Catholic cathedral was attended not only by Orthodox and Armenian Christians but also by Jews.

During the Second World War the belligerents regarded Istanbul as neutral territory, but there tensions were high. Angelo had to tread carefully, taking care to remember, as he wrote, that the Church, as 'the mother of all nations', should not take sides in the war. He deplored the Italian invasion of Greece, which was followed by a German assault, yet he ministered to the occupying forces as well as remaining in close contact with Greek Christians. He struck up a relationship with the German ambassador, Franz von Papen, as well as with Baron Kurt von Lerner, whom he respected as a Protestant anti-Nazi; he kept open channels with the French supporters of Pétain and the French resistance; he helped to persuade the allies to lift a blockade of Greece during the winter famine of 1941; he played his part in the deals to enable Jews to escape from the Nazis throughout Istanbul. (Not surprisingly, therefore, when he celebrated his first Good Friday Mass as pope he deleted from the liturgy unseemly but long-accepted words insulting to Jews.)

Numerous people flattered him by suggesting that he was destined for yet greater things. He resisted the temptation to believe them, treating their words as a joke. But a new post was waiting for him. On 6 December 1944 a telegram arrived on his desk from the Vatican. It ordered the archbishop to leave Istanbul for Paris, as the newly appointed nuncio to the government of France. Bemused, indeed amazed that the Holy Father should have so much honoured him, Roncalli packed his bags and arrived in France as the new year was breaking. And he found a Church in conflict with itself, his predecessor expelled by General de Gaulle for his wartime support of the Vichy régime and another thirty or so bishops under suspicion as collaborators.

Roncalli managed to reduce the number of bishops to be expelled to three. Twenty-seven new bishops were appointed, all of them through Roncalli's diplomatic skills rendered acceptable to the French government. Once every two weeks, in order to smooth the affairs of the Church, he had a private meeting with Georges Bidault, the leader of the Popular Republican Movement, a man whom Roncalli personally disliked. More congenial to him were the atheist socialist Vincent Auriol and the speaker of the national assembly, Edouard Herriot, himself also an unbeliever. Roncalli also became a close friend of another Popular Republican Movement leader, Robert Schumann.

This apparent Italian dumbskull was insinuating himself into the highest circles of French diplomacy. He travelled across France and also visited the French territories in northern Africa. He read voraciously, taking in the radical thinking of French Catholic scholars, and being in Paris he also ate with equal devotion. (When he became pope, those invited to eat with him were delighted to be served splendid food and equally splendid wine.)

In matters of theology his master in the Vatican was less pliant. Though adventurous where Biblical scholarship was concerned, the pope disliked the progressive views of such scholars as Henri de Lubac and Yves Congar, and both were eventually forbidden to publish their speculations. Roncalli reluctantly obeyed the papal directives about them, and the two scholars were sent into intellectual exile.

At the end of 1952 Pius XII made the Archbishop Angelo Roncalli a cardinal. Early in the following year, on 15 January, a letter arrived from the Vatican informing the archbishop that he must leave Paris to become Patriarch of Venice. It was an honour, Roncalli declared, far beyond his deserts.

The future pope was now seventy-one years old. Soon, he thought, he must die. His will was no longer suited to his new exalted position, so he changed it, decreeing that his body should be laid in the cathedral of San Marco, close by the tomb of the disciple of St Peter, the evangelist Mark himself. Arrived at the city, he made a public address in which he proudly proclaimed his humble origins. 'I derive from a modest family, brought up in happy and blessed poverty – poverty which demands little but fosters the most honest and the highest virtues, preparing one for life's greatest adventures.' He rejoiced, he said, to have encountered different religions and ideologies. Now that he was back in his homeland, he wished to be simply a brother who would be loving, approachable and understanding. 'So,' he concluded, 'you perceive that I am a simple man.' And in Venice he said, 'I wish to be a real pastor.'

The patriarch still mused about his elevated station and the comparative lowliness of his family. 'I must love them, especially because they are poor,' he wrote in 1955, 'but I must also live a life separated from them, to set a good example to the priests of my diocese, some of whom, sometimes excusably, surround themselves with too many relations.'

For six years he served the city, hosting parties for artists who exhibited at the Venice Biennale, welcoming the composer Igor Stravinsky into his cathedral (for a performance of Stravinsky's *Sacred Canticle in honour of St Mark the Evangelist*) and, in a less major but still important decision, declaring that when women came into his cathedral, they and not the cathedral authorities should decide what it was fitting for them to wear. This last judgement, seemingly trivial, revealed this man as one who trusted the laity to think for themselves.

His apostolic superior, Pope Pius XII, was not totally supportive of the patriarch. Pius XII was adamant that the patriarch should distance himself from the Venetian socialists. He insisted that Roncalli forbid his priests and lay people to vote communist. Archbishop Roncalli scrupulously obeyed the pope's orders, yet somehow managed to welcome the Italian socialist congress when it convened in Venice in 1957. As he said in his address, 'a decent Venetian offers hospitality.' He was sharp enough to condemn the anticlericalism of some members of the congress, but at the same time he acknowledged that many participants desired to promote goodness, justice and peace.

At the age of seventy-six, Angelo Roncalli had a premonition. He wrote in his diary, 'The Lord Jesus, I think, has in store for me before I die some great suffering and affliction of body and spirit for my complete mortification and purification, so as to admit me to his eternal joy.' One year later Pius XII died. In mid-October Angelo Roncalli arrived in Rome. On 25 October he was at the conclave to elect the next pope. Some of his friends hinted that the next pope might have been born in Bergamo.

'That matters nothing,' said Angelo Roncalli. But he must have known that he was the favourite, though by no means a certainty as next pope, for Cardinals Gregory Agaganian and Alfredo Ottaviani were also strongly favoured. In an act of delicate reparation, he himself voted for the cardinal Charles de

Gaulle had managed to have expelled from his see in Paris. As Roncalli later confided to his diary, he did nothing to advance his own cause as the next pope and even rejoiced as the voters seemed to favour other candidates. But at the eleventh ballot, on 28 October, in his seventy-seventh year, he was elected.

In truth he had prepared a speech for the occasion. He would call himself Pope John, since (as we have noted) that was the name of his father and the dedication of the parish church in which he was baptised. In addition, he said, almost every one of his twenty-two predecessors had reigned only for a short time. Finally, he fully expected that both St John the Baptist and the disciple named John who leaned on Jesus's breast at the Last Supper would pray for him in his new task.

John XXIII appointed Domenico Tardini as his secretary of state, raising him to the rank of cardinal. He summoned the clergy of his new diocese to a synod, where this radical man displayed his love of tradition by insisting that always the men of God should publicly wear cassocks and submit to the tonsure. He believed the priesthood to be an exceedingly special calling, incompatible, for instance, with toil in the workplace, and it was John XXIII who stopped the worker–priest movement.

He was to confide to his diary that there was a widespread belief in the 1958 conclave that the cardinals had elected him as a provisional, transitional pope. By then, he added, he was in his fourth year as supreme pontiff, with an immense programme before him.

Almost instantly, where his predecessors had dithered, the new pope had summoned the Second Vatican Council. He commanded it at the beginning of 1959 (and his secretary of state Tardini supposed that he had experienced a brief period of madness). Its aim he defined as the promotion of the reunion of all the separated Christian communities. It was to be an ecumenical council. Its theme, the theme of John XXIII's entire ministry as pope, would be *aggiornamento* – renewal.

On hearing his announcement, the assembled cardinals were dumbfounded. They sent Cardinal Tardini to remonstrate with the pope – in the politest possible way – by suggesting that any public announcement of the intended council be delayed. They also feared that any approach to non-Catholic Churches would compromise the position of the papacy and also contradict the whole thrust of the reign of Pius XII. The pope agreed to postpone publication of his decision. Diplomatically, he also allowed the cardinals of the Roman curia to head the commissions set up to prepare for his council.

The Orthodox, Anglican and Protestant Churches were delighted. Athenagoras, Patriarch of Constantinople, expressed his joy. Geoffrey Fisher, Archbishop of Canterbury, went further in December 1960, by paying what he called a courtesy visit to the pope. Fisher was a determined ecumenicist, though in no sense one who brushed aside theological differences. He had already begged the Free Churches to 'take episcopacy into their own system'. He met the pope on his return from the Middle East, where he had visited leaders of the Orthodox Churches, such as the Patriarch of Jerusalem and the Ecumenical Patriarch Athenagoras I.

Fisher's move was a bold one. He once confessed that he grew up with an inbred opposition to anything that came from Rome. 'I objected to their doctrine; I objected to their methods of reasoning; I objected to their methods of operation in this country.' Roman Catholics in Britain could be equally intransigent. When in 1956 Christians gathered in the Albert Hall to express their sympathy with the Hungarians who had been invaded by Soviet Russia, the Catholic authorities had objected to the plan that Fisher should give a blessing in the presence of a Roman Catholic archbishop, and the Catholic prelate left before the blessing was given.

With the advent of John XXIII this bitter atmosphere was transformed, and Archbishop Fisher said so. What changed everything, he declared, was 'Without any doubt, the personality of Pope John.' He added, 'It was quite obvious to the world that Pope John was a different kind of Pope, whom I should like to meet, and could meet, on grounds of Christian brotherhood without any kind of ecclesiastical compromise on either side.'

So there took place the first meeting between a pope and an Archbishop of Canterbury since Archbishop Arundel visited the Vatican in 1397. Tardini was ill-pleased, going so far as to send the official Vatican photographer on holiday. There was one notable exchange. John XXIII expressed his wish that the separated Churches should return to the mother Church. 'Your Holiness, not *return*,' responded Fisher. 'None of us can go backwards. We are each now running on parallel courses; we are looking forward until, in God's good time, our two courses approximate and meet.' According to Fisher's account, after a moment's pause the pope replied, 'You are right.' Maybe he did.

The Second Vatican Council first met towards the end of 1962. In the meantime every one of the Church's three thousand bishops and archbishops had been invited to make suggestions for its agenda (as had 156 heads of religious orders and Catholic theological faculties). The new pope believed both in papal supremacy and also in 'collegiality' – that one of his briefs was to express the collegial will of the whole Church and that it was valuable to have a consensus amongst Christians before any dogmatic pronouncement should be made.

Though some of the bishops who submitted their ideas wanted nothing to do with non-Catholics, the pope also wished to hold out his hand to the separated brethren of Christianity:

Protestants, Anglicans and those members of the Eastern Orthodox Churches who were not in communion with Rome. As he had said on leaving Bulgaria:

> 'Wherever I may go in the world, should anyone from Bulgaria pass my house at night in distress, he will find a light in my window. Knock knock! I shall not ask whether you are a Catholic or not. Enter, my Bulgarian brother, and two fraternal arms will welcome you. A friend's warm heart will rejoice that you have come.'

Such too should now have a place in the Second Vatican Council. To this end Cardinal Augustin Bea was told to set up a secretariat for Christian unity. Energetically, Bea supported his master, even sending a lieutenant to the hitherto scorned World Council of Churches.

The First Vatican Council had welcomed fewer than a dozen African bishops, all of whom had been born in Europe. The second welcomed three hundred, a tenth of whom had been born outside Europe. And Latin American bishops, a tiny minority in 1870, now numbered some six hundred. Altogether Pope John XXIII created fifty-four new ones. No pope before him had created an African or an Indian cardinal.

Another innovation was to invite 'observers' from other Churches: Orthodox Christians (represented only by those sent from Russia), Anglicans, Lutherans, Calvinists, Quakers, Methodists and other Protestants. Pope John XXIII decided that they should have the best seats at the council, observing that to Jesus belonged not simply the children of the Catholic Church but all those baptized in his name – indeed, every person created by God. Beleaguered Catholics from the Soviet bloc were also represented, for the communist authorities allowed bishops from

Eastern Germany, from Hungary, from Czechoslovakia, from Yugoslavia and from Poland to attend.

In his short reign this pope issued two major encyclicals: *Mater et Magistra* and *Pacem in terris* (as well as *Princeps pastorum*, which was devoted to Christian missions and expressed his concern for the under-developed countries of the world). The first of his major encyclicals offered just praise to the social teaching of Leo XIII's revolutionary *Rerum novarum*. His own aim, wrote John XXIII, was merely to develop the views set out by Leo XIII. He went far beyond it, commending free state education and hospitals as the right of everyone. Everyone, too, he insisted, should have the right to work and also to recreation. His encyclical condemned grinding poverty, but also insisted on the dignity of the life of a peasant-farmer. As for industrial workers, the pope declared that they should wherever possible have some share in the profits of the firms for which they worked. And everyone, he insisted, had the right to participate in public life.

John XXIII reinforced this message in a broadcast speech of 11 September 1962. The Church, he pronounced, was the Church of the poor. Its duty was to speak out against the miseries of social life which cry out for God's vengeance. He affirmed the fundamental equality of all people. He believed, as he put it in his speech opening Vatican II, that Providence was leading mankind towards a new order in human relations.

In religious matters, *Pacem in terris* was yet more radical. Already in Venice Angelo Roncalli had insisted that Church unity must derive from charity, rather than dogma, and – unfashionably for that time – he declared that little charity had been displayed on the Catholic as well as the Protestant side. *Pacem in terris* openly advocated religious freedom, the right of anyone to believe and worship according to his or her conscience.

He addressed it not solely to Catholics or even Christians but 'to all men of good will'. His ecumenical council furthered the idea, inviting what the pope called 'separated communities' (not heretical Churches) to participate in order to promote the unity which almost all Christians desired.

Curiously, this did not in his view diminish his own status as pope, for in this encyclical he described himself as the interpreter of the wishes of the whole human family and spoke of his fatherly love for all of humanity. These included communists, a clear change from the hard line of his predecessor, though the new pope still found communism distasteful. The Soviet leader Nikita Khrushchev responded to his warmth, allowing clergy under his control to attend Vatican II and sending (or, perhaps, allowing) his son-in-law, Aleksei Adzhubei, to visit the pope. These contacts led to a distinct thaw in relations between the Soviets and the Churches under their sway. Imprisoned priests were released and one of the most important of these was Archbishop Slipyi of Lwow.

The wealthy nations, John XXIII believed, should render every possible assistance to the less developed ones. Racialism he completely outlawed. And by now even the erroneous philosophy of communism (as he described it) seemed to him to contain elements that he could commend. Though the pope did not condemn war as a means to remedy injustice, the nuclear race between east and west was, his encyclical said, regrettable, and the nations should seek a ban on nuclear tests, followed by a ban on nuclear warfare and a closely monitored disarmament.

This was a delightful man. John XXIII had a sly wit, which he used to good effect. He once said that if he had any problem he first thought he would ask the pope about it, until he remembered that he *was* the pope, and decided to ask God about it instead. Another cunning jest forced Cardinal Amleto Cicognani to accept the post of secretary of state after the death of Domenico Tardini. Cicognani did not want the post. He was aged and sick, he protested. He needed time to think about it. Pope John chattered about other matters for half-an-hour. Then he observed that the cardinal had been given time to think and must now take the job. The cardinal accepted.

He was also a pastoral pope, stunning the general public not only by visiting Rome's gaol, but also its hospitals for children. Although pope, this man remained humble to the end. Visiting Pius XII, many felt constrained to address him on their knees (it was even said that some fell to their knees when he telephoned them). John XXIII could not bear this obsequiousness and stopped the practice.

In November 1961 the first twinges of cancer of the stomach beset him. Soon his doctors confined him to bed, yet he survived till the end of the following year. In his last year on earth the pope decided to give fewer luncheons, and his habitual glasses of wine were abandoned. Being elderly, he had hoped that the council he had convened would not last long, finished, perhaps, in a single session. His hope was unrealisable. John XXIII's legacy to his successor in the chair of St Peter was to continue Vatican II.

Originally it was planned that the second session of the Council should open in May 1963. In that month the pope left the Vatican for the last time, visiting the Quirinal to receive the Balzan peace prize. He continued to receive heads of the separated Churches: Canadian Anglicans, French Protestants, British Methodists.

His death was painful, and his final sufferings lasted three days. Protestants and Orthodox as well as Catholics prayed, to no avail, that he might survive. The pope was sanguine: as he put it, quoting Ecclesiastes, there is a time to be born and a time for dying. As he had written in his private journal at the age of twenty-one, 'I like to enjoy good health, but if God sends me sickness, well, blessed be this sickness!' He even joked that in one month the Vatican could both be rid of one pope and have elected another.

His influence had been immense. 'No four years of papal history have seen such major policy changes as Pope John made,' wrote the Catholic historian E. E. Y. Hales. 'During his short reign he reversed both the international and the Italian policy of the Papacy.' He even left his mark on the basilica of St Peter in Rome by inviting Giacomo Manzu, who came from his own Bergamo region, to design a new bronze door for the cathedral.

Were there any precedents for this remarkable pope? Perhaps Benedict XV, a totally different man in many ways, comes closest. 'It is beyond doubt that Pope Benedict XV's message of pacifism suffered only a temporary eclipse from totalitarian warmongering,' judged the astute historian Carlo Falconi. 'It took the horrors of the Second World War, and the inadequate conduct of Pius XII in relation to them, to cause that message to be revalued at its true worth.' Falconi added: 'If, in fact, any pontificate foreshadowed and prepared the way for the miracle of John XXIII, the robust and genial Bergamesque peasant, it is that of the frail, reserved Genoese aristocrat, Giacomo della Chiesa.'

On Whit Monday John XXIII frequently lapsed into unconsciousness. He died on the evening of that same day, at ten minutes before eight. And when his yellow corpse was carried into St Peter's Square, the huge crowd gasped and began to weep. Today, in the crypt of St Peter's, Rome, few gather round the tombs of other popes, but pilgrims always surround that of John XXIII. His tomb is constantly covered with flowers.

CHAPTER SEVEN

Paul VI

John XXIII once described his successor as pope, Cardinal Giovanni Battista Enrico Antonio Maria Montini, as 'somewhat like Hamlet'. It was a shrewd remark, and many of the acts of Montini as pope confirmed the judgement. He often vacillated: warming to non-Roman Catholic Churches, yet deeply concerned not to jeopardise his own papal authority; fully aware that women in the Church had in the past been relegated to subordinate roles, as if their supreme role as mothers justified this, yet opposed to any moves to ordain them priests; able to issue decisive encyclicals, particularly his controversial *Humanae Vitae*, yet deeply hurt when the outside world, and particularly other Christians, rejected his views.

The successor of John XXIII had also suffered some papal insults in his life. To outsiders this may not have seemed to be the case, but when Pius XII moved him from Rome to the archbishopric of Milan, Montini was effectively snubbed by the fact that he was not then made a cardinal, considered inevitable with that post.

John XXIII had reversed this insult, particularly as – unlike some – Montini had welcomed the notion of a Second Vatican Council, which would be devoted to the union of nations, to the welfare of the poor, to progress, to justice and to liberty.

His parents, Giorgio Montini and Giudetta Alghisi, had met in Rome in 1883, outside the basilica of St Peter, where both had received the papal blessing of Leo XIII. Giorgio, aged thirty-three, edited a Catholic newspaper, *Il Cittadino di Brescia.* Giudetta, fourteen years his junior, was ward of the mayor of Brescia, an anti-clerical friend of Garibaldi. The two defied the opposition of the mayor, and when she reached the age of twenty-one they married. The future pope, their second son, was born on 26 September 1897.

Battista Montini was brought up by a wet-nurse, and lived with her in a cottage in Peretti, just outside Brescia. Whenever he returned home, he played with the children of his father's tenants. Three years after he was born, his mother gave birth to a third son. Theirs was a religious home, and his father inaugurated the erection of a statue of Jesus on Monte Guiglielmo to mark the turn of the twentieth century.

The boy was taught by Jesuits. He was also educated by his literary parents (his mother taught him French) and subconsciously by the many important guests at his parents' table, the journalists and intellectuals of Brescia. As he grew older, he and his brothers also benefited from the intellectual Oratorians who ran the church of Santa Maria della Pace in Brescia. In 1965, as Paul VI, Battista made one of these, Giulio Bevilacqua, with whom he had often cycled through the countryside, a cardinal.

And, unlike the families of his predecessors, this child had been born into a line which had easy access to the papacy. In 1907, the three children were taken by their parents (and his mother's sister) for a private audience with Pope Pius X.

Battista Montini loved cycling, and the passion nearly ended his life. During one outing the young man suffered a mild heart attack. In consequence he was increasingly educated by private tutors, since attending school was deemed too strenuous. Meanwhile Benedictines from France with their superb liturgy were inspiring in him a love of the Church, and this prompted his first desires for the priesthood. And as he studied for his vocation he profited from his father's profession by editing a student magazine, *La Fionda* (*The Sling*), which attempted to preach to Catholic students a gospel capable of coping with the horrors of the First World War.

In 1919 he went on retreat to the famous monastery of Monte Cassino, and then set off on the road to ordination. When at the age of twenty-two he became a priest, on 19 May 1920, his mother unfolded her own wedding dress and had it made into a chasuble for her son. As for his father, Giorgio Montini arranged that his son should not take the post of a humble parish priest but study literature at the Sapienza University in Rome, in preparation for taking a doctorate in Church history.

At first he studied at the Lombardy Seminary, but once again his family connections decided that this was not good enough, and soon, through the influence of Cardinal Pietro Gasparri, he was transferred to the Academy for Noble Ecclesiastics, which trained the papal diplomats. As he put it, he was instantly transformed from a student to a future man of affairs.

His first mission was to visit newly-created Poland, which had expelled the Bolsheviks in 1920 and was now a nation busily, indeed alarmingly, expanding itself at the expense of its neighbours. Montini reached Warsaw in June 1923. Though Poland was a predominantly Catholic country, nearly one third of the city's population was Jewish.

Battista, who had failed to learn German properly, was baffled by the Polish language and mostly communicated with the Polish in French. He met Marshal Joséf Pilsudki and the primate of Poland, visited Czestochowa, with its famous black icon of the Virgin Mary, and made pastoral visits to Gdansk and Poznan.

But his heart was not in the work and his health was still poor. Through his family connections he tried to have himself recalled to Italy, and eventually he succeeded. On 13 October 1923 he was back in Rome, to take up the post of chaplain (along with others) to its Catholic students. His and their problems (especially as he came from a politically liberal family) were greatly aggravated by the rise of Mussolini's fascists, whose values he deplored.

Soon Montini was confronted with fascist mobs attacking loyal Catholic students and by the end of the year the fascists had outlawed all other political parties. Montini witnessed their brutality at first hand in future years, when anti-fascist students in his care were sometimes beaten up. He also was saddened to see his father's newspaper closed down. Soon the fascists would ban all Italian Catholic youth movements.

Battista Montini now preferred to holiday in France, rather than in Poland, living there with Benedictines, making contact with French Catholic intellectuals – particularly the brilliant Jacques Maritain and the propagandist and memorialist Jean Guitton. Soon he was back in Rome with a new job, as under-secretary of state to the pope, with Cardinal Gasparri as his boss. Later he was to visit Belgium and Germany, declining a tour of the Middle East on the grounds of ill-health. In the summer of 1934 he holidayed in Britain and the Irish republic, visiting and admiring some nine Anglican cathedrals and marvelling at the organ music which enriched them – though he also voiced a Roman prejudice that Christ was absent and that there was no priesthood and no faith. The Catholics of Scotland and Ireland impressed him more.

With the new title of Monsignor, from 1926 to 1933 he continued to work as national chaplain to the federation of Italian Catholic university students and wrote regularly for the student magazines. He translated into Italian Jacques Maritain's book *Three Reformers* (which discussed from a sympathetic, yet staunchly Catholic viewpoint, Martin Luther, René Descartes and Jean-Jacques Rousseau).

His background made him sceptical about the Lateran Pacts, whereas when they were signed Pius XI declared, 'Providence put Mussolini in our path.' Montini's own circle was, he noted, 'filled with reservations and forebodings.' Yet Pius XI now welcomed the King and Queen of Italy into the Vatican. These differences did not, however, impede the future pope's career. Soon Battista Montini would be appointed secretary to Eugenio Pacelli, by now the pope's secretary of state. And when Pacelli became pope, Battista was destined for even higher office.

He found Pacelli a kind man, who once sent him five bottles of wine on his feast day, and he assisted with Pacelli's attempts to avert the Second World War, partly drafting the pope's August appeal for peace in 1939.

Montini recorded some of the pope's hesitations about speaking out against Nazi and fascist aggression: 'what restrains me,' said the pope, 'is the fear of making worse the plight of the victims.' Yet, as Montini also noted, at times the whole world longed for him to speak. Nonetheless, Montini for the rest of his life continued to defend his patron's actions as wholly justified.

Soon, when Italy entered the war on the German side, the Vatican city became the refuge of all the diplomats of the allies, and most of them came into contact with Montini, who was frequently exhausted and close to suffering a nervous breakdown. These diplomats also encountered high-ranking Vatican officials who openly sympathised with fascism. Montini did not, either openly or privately, and in consequence came under attack not only from them (particularly Cardinal Nicola Canali, governor of the Vatican city state) but also from political circles close to Mussolini, including Count Galeazzo Ciano, Italian foreign minister and Mussolini's son-in-law. He wrote home that, although he was also attacked by the fascist press, he had a clear conscience and also the support of his superiors. His strength came especially, he told his family, from the support and help of Pius XII himself.

Though he took the greatest care to appear impartial, no one could disguise the fact that his politics as a young man had been firmly aligned with the *Partito Popolare Italiano*, whose sometime leader, Alcide de Gasperi, had remained his friend up to and throughout the Mussolini era. De Gasperi and others (such as another friend, the future premier of Italy, Aldo Moro) had schemes for a new, Christian Democratic party to rule the country once the war was over, and Battista Montini sympathised with this. Two years after the war had ended, his views prevailed in the Vatican.

Western Church leaders now increasingly visited Rome for audiences with the pope, and many of them thus came into contact with Montini. Ecumenicism was in the air, and in 1948 the World Council of Churches was set up in Amsterdam. The Council set up its headquarters in Geneva and eventually would embrace over two hundred Churches – Orthodox, Protestant and Anglican. But neither Pius XII nor the Patriarch of Moscow sent emissaries to Amsterdam.

During the Holy Year of 1950, Battista Montini remained a

loyal servant of the pope. In December he was busy with the organisation of a world congress of the lay apostolate, which was scheduled for 1951. Early in 1953 when the pope held only the second consistory of his reign, in order to name new cardinals, many confidently expected Montini to be one of them, but it was not to be. It appeared he had been slighted by Pius XII, for Montini had no chance of succeeding him as the next pope. And when the Cardinal Archbishop of Milan died in the same year, Pius XII appointed Montini to succeed him as archbishop, but not as cardinal. Milan was a prestigious see, but to many it seemed that the pope's sometime favourite had been exiled.

Now, however, this man who had never been a parish priest threw himself into the pastoral work of the diocese. He tried to make himself approachable to the estranged working class. He urged the building of new churches. Of course he also returned to Rome – particularly for the second world congress of the lay apostolate, which was held in 1957, where he did his usual balancing act between tradition and renewal. He also urged his listeners to love both friends and enemies, defining them (amongst others) as Catholics, schismatics, Protestants, Anglicans, the indifferent, Muslims, pagans and atheists. His speech reaped much applause. And in his see he continued to welcome those from other Churches willing to seek him.

The death of Pius XII and the election as pope of Battista Montini's old friend Angelo Giuseppe Roncalli remedied the injustice of Pius XII's refusal to grant the Archbishop of Milan a cardinal's hat. The new pope made Montini his first cardinal. When Roncalli announced that he was to call the Second Vatican Council, Montini told his diocese that it would be the greatest the Church had ever held.

Indeed the accession of John XXIII seemed to have liberated him. Montini no longer seemed to feel the need to equivocate in his pronouncements, as he had so frequently done under Pius XII. At the new pope's suggestion he travelled abroad more often, visiting the United States of America, Southern Rhodesia, Nigeria and Ghana.

In June 1963 he was at the dying pope's bedside, before returning to Milan. Eighty-one cardinals arrived in Rome for the conclave to elect John XXIII's successor. The first votes put Montini ahead, but not with the necessary two-thirds majority. Only on the sixth ballot, which gave him fifty-seven votes, was Montini elected.

At the age of sixty-six on 30 June he was crowned Pope Paul VI. He took the name Paul, because, like St Paul, he wished to support a mission to the Gentiles. Rome, in the new pope's view, was not only the city of authority, truth and catholicity, but also of love and unity. His pontificate welcomed such august figures as Metropolitan Nikodim of Leningrad and the Anglican Franciscan scholar Bishop John Moorman of Ripon. Yet more radically, it saw the establishment of a secretariat for atheists.

His major task was to continue with the Second Vatican Council, which was to reconvene at the end of September. His speech to it was startlingly ecumenical. He acknowledged the riches of truth and spirituality possessed by 'our separated brethren'. Yet more surprisingly, he declared that, 'If we are in any way to blame for our prolonged separation, we humbly beg God's forgiveness and also ask pardon of our brethren who feel they have been injured by us.' Thirdly, he willingly forgave the injuries done to the Catholic Church and was ready to forget the grief caused by the long dissensions and separations.

Freed from the shackles of Pius XII, Montini was now willing to find some accommodation even with what he called the 'blind dogma' of atheistic communism. He believed that time was on the side of the Church, whose teachings would eventually prevail. But he also stressed that individual communists, who had hitherto suffered the harshness of Christians, ought also to feel the Church's love. In this regard, he was both sustained and influenced by Pope John XXIII.

Paul VI remained faithful to John XXIII above all by taking over and fostering his ecumenical council. Its results continued to be momentous, even in such matters as the Catholic liturgy. After the Second Vatican Council no longer would the priest celebrate Holy Communion with his back turned for most of the time towards the laity. This change was probably one that John XXIII would have welcomed. As Archbishop of Venice, Angelo Roncalli had attempted and failed to remove the Iconastasis, a marble screen that makes it impossible for worshippers to see the priests consecrating the Blessed Sacrament at the high altar. In the debates of the bishops preparing for the Second Vatican Council, Battista Montini had spoken out for a liturgy expressed in the vernacular and not necessarily always celebrated in Latin. In justification, the pope would quote St Augustine's dictum that it was better to speak ungrammatically, if the people understood, than to speak learnedly and not be understood at all.

Artificial contraception (as contrasted with the so-called rhythm method approved of by Pius XII) was a different matter. On this subject, the pope vacillated. He had set up an advisory committee of experts, the majority of whom declared in favour of contraception. On his own authority (and almost certainly pushed this way by Cardinal Wojtyla of Krakow) the pope rejected their finding, declaring contraception to be unacceptable. His encyclical *Humanae Vitae* went so far as to proclaim that it opened the way to marital infidelity and a progressive lowering of sexual standards. At the very beginning of human life, declared the pope, human existence must be defended. He also added that those who sought to impose birth control on married couples were intervening in the most personal and intimate responsibility of a man and his wife (as if, in some way, his encyclical was not doing precisely that).

Many scrutinized the encyclical for buried signs of tolerance – and found them, in particular in a sentence that offered liberty to priests and laity: 'Husbands and wives,' said Paul VI in this his most controversial encyclical, 'when they are deeply distressed by the difficulties of their lives, must find stamped in the heart and words of their priest the same voice and love of our Saviour.' Some, both priests and layfolk, took this as an opening to ignore *Humanae Vitae*. Even so, a few leading churchmen, such as Cardinal Archbishop Léon-Joseph Suenens of Belgium, openly presumed to criticise the pope for ignoring the principle of collegiality.

Yet Paul VI was equally adamant over the question of clerical celibacy. He specifically forbade the council to discuss the subject. His intention, as he wrote to Cardinal Eugène Tisserant, was not simply to preserve the ancient rule but also to strengthen its observance. After the council was over, his encyclical *Sacerdotalis coelibatus* reaffirmed the principle of celibacy for the Catholic clergy.

This encyclical incorporated three buried grenades, waiting to explode at some time in the future. First, it necessarily had to admit that clerical celibacy was not imposed until the eleventh century of the Christian era. Secondly, equally clearly, many Orthodox clergy (whose legitimate priesthood was not denied by the Vatican) were married, unless they were bishops. Thirdly, ministerial converts from other Churches who were already married might well be offered the privilege of exercising the sacred ministry.

Soon the encyclical was challenged even by high-ranking

ecclesiastics inside the pope's own communion. Many Dutch bishops in particular believed that celibacy should not be imposed on the clergy and that the time was ripe for ordaining as priests married men. According to these Dutch bishops, even priests who had begun their ministries vowed to celibacy ought, if they so wished, to be allowed to marry. They also held that some of those priests ejected from the ministry for marrying should be reinstated. Yet the pope was faced by a contrary view, led amongst others by Cardinal Wojtyla of Krakow and the brilliant conservative theologian Cardinal Josef Ratzinger. Paul VI was leading a seriously divided Church.

The pope ended the third session of Vatican II dramatically, with the announcement that he was planning a visit to the Holy Land. His visit would further his ecumenicism. There he met the Greek Orthodox Patriarch of Jerusalem, as well as Lutherans and Anglicans. But his chief desire was to open up public relations with the Ecumenical Patriarch of Constantinople, Athenagoras II, who told him, in the church of the Holy Sepulchre, that they should demonstrate to the whole world that they were once again brothers. The pope gave Athenagoras a chalice; the Ecumenical Patriarch gave the pope a pectoral cross.

Then he visited India, which he described as the cradle of great religions. There he appealed to the wealthy nations to abandon the arms race and concentrate on eliminating poverty and need in the developing countries. His subsequent encyclical, *Populorum Progressio*, insisted that the wealthy had an obligation to feed the hungry and care for the health of every member of the human race. 'The superfluous wealth of the rich nations,' he wrote, 'must be put to the benefit of the poor ones.'

Paul VI was back in Rome for the final session of the Second Vatican Council, which began in mid-September 1965, the same year in which his friend Aldo Moro had become premier of

Italy. The pope crammed into this last session a lightning, thirty-six-hour visit to the United States of America, where he met President Lyndon B. Johnson and visited the headquarters of the United Nations. Here he insisted that the nations, instead of supporting artificial contraception, which would 'cut down the number of guests at the banquet of life', must so much improve the production of food as to provide enough for everyone.

When the Second Vatican Council finally closed its doors, the pope decided on his second visit to Catholic and communist Poland. Its bishops, led by Cardinal Archbishop Stefan Wyszynski and buttressed intellectually by Archbishop Karol Wojtyla, had made a forceful impact on Paul VI during the council. The anniversary year 1966 was approaching, which would mark one thousand years from the establishment of Polish Christianity. The Polish Catholics planned to carry the icon of the Black Virgin of Czestochowa throughout their land. In May many of them wished Pope Paul VI to celebrate Mass at Czestochowa. Wyszynski was not amongst those who supported this idea, planning to preside over the millennium celebrations himself, and – deliberately or not – he so managed to offend the Polish government that it was made clear that the pope was not welcome for the millennium. Wyszynski presided over the celebrations.

The pope's relations with communist Hungary were complicated by the extraordinary fact that the Budapest government had accused the primate of Hungary, Cardinal Josef Mindszenty, of treason and in 1949 sentenced him to life imprisonment. In 1955 the Vatican had secured his release, with the condition that he stayed in Hungary. Mindszenty took refuge in the American legation, a voluntary prisoner there till the papacy secured his return to Rome in 1971, Pope Paul's emissaries having argued that the cardinal's delicate health might lead to an embarrassing death in the legation.

Paul VI suggested that Mindszenty should remain quiet over the internal problems of Hungary and its relationships with the Holy See, and that he should not publish his memoirs. Initially, to the chagrin of Paul VI, Mindszenty indignantly refused these conditions, and it was with some difficulty that he was persuaded to leave the legation and come to Rome.

Other radical ventures proved far more successful. In particular, in March 1966 Michael Ramsey, Archbishop of Canterbury, visited Rome and was publicly welcomed by the pope in the Sistine Chapel. 'This is your home,' said the pope, 'where you have a right to be.' Later the same afternoon they met privately. Michael Ramsey was both a distinguished theologian (an Anglo-Catholic) and a man of prayer. So he and Paul VI spoke about both matters. Should not the papacy reconsider the question of Anglican orders, so brusquely dismissed in Leo XIII's bull *Apostolicae Curae*? Would it not be possible to translate the Lord's Prayer and the creeds in ways acceptable to both Anglicans and Catholics?

Beneath his quaint exterior, Archbishop Ramsey concealed considerable steeliness. Why, he asked, did the Catholic Church rebaptise converts who had been validly baptised in Anglican churches? Why was Rome so rigid about mixed marriages, insisting that these take place invariably in Catholic churches and that any children be brought up strictly as Catholics? When they met again, in the basilica of St Paul Without the Walls, the pope slipped his episcopal ring on the archbishop's finger. Ramsey gave Paul VI a pectoral cross. And, more important perhaps, they resolved to set up a joint Anglican–Catholic theological commission.

Since that meeting Pope Paul VI never ceased to hold

Anglicanism in high honour. Even when he canonised forty English and Welsh Catholics martyred at the Reformation (an act some could have seen as provocative to the Anglican Church), he declared that their blood might be effective in healing the wound inflicted on the Church of God by the separation of the Anglican Church and the Catholic Church; for – as he on that occasion declared – the Roman Church regarded the Anglican as 'her ever-beloved sister.' This was a long way from regarding Anglicans as heretics.

Paul VI visited Turkey in mid-1967, to present his respects to the Ecumenical Patriarch Athenagoras II, who visited Rome in September of the same year. The pope explicitly said that his flock and the Orthodox community were 'sister Churches'. By now the pope was not well, but he bore his afflictions (in particular an enlarged prostate gland and the need to wear a catheter) with equanimity. After his operation he convalesced and recuperated in time to meet President Lyndon B. Johnson two days before Christmas. The following year he made the first visit of any pope to Latin America.

In Bogotá he ordained some two hundred priests and deacons; in Medellín he faced up to the problems of Brazil, aided by Dom Helder Camara (Archbishop of Olinda–Recife) whom he had known for decades and whose denunciations of institutionalised repression and corruption had endeared him to many outside as well as inside Catholicism.

Paul VI's next major visit was to the World Council of Churches in Geneva. He conceded no papal claim (indeed, he puzzled many of the members by telling them that his name was Peter!), but it was a significant move from the papal point of view. One month later, in July 1969, he was in Africa, to visit at Namungongo the shrine of the martyrs of Uganda, young Christian men murdered by the Kabanga, deposed by president

Milton Obote in 1967. In the country's capital, Kampala, he also met other African leaders, including the Catholic president of Tanzania, Julius Nyerere. Although these meetings contributed little of note to African and papal policy, the pope was chalking up a considerable number of firsts. And one phrase he used was keenly noted: Africa, while resisting any synthesis of Catholicism with local religions, must develop a truly 'African Christianity'.

Paul VI did not cease travelling abroad. In 1972 he would in a mere ten days visit Teheran, Karachi, the Philippines, Samoa, Australia (here celebrating Mass on Randwick racecourse), Jakarta, Hong Kong (where he stayed for three hours and twenty-five minutes, including a Mass, also celebrated at the racecourse) and Sri Lanka. And on this foreign tour he almost lost his life. In the airport of Manila a deranged Bolivian, Benjamin Mendoza y Amor, attempted to kill the pope with a double-edged knife. The papal entourage overpowered Mendoza, and on the spot Paul VI forgave him.

Paul VI followed the example of his predecessors and decided to proclaim a Holy Year in 1975, which attracted countless pilgrims to Rome. Yet his primacy continued to be beset with some holy and some far from holy problems. The Vatican Bank was losing money. In the pope's view the Jesuits needed disciplining. He was concerned that the Anglican Church was contemplating the ordination of women priests.

And he was greatly disturbed by the rebellion of the French Archbishop Marcel Lefebvre against virtually everything enshrined in Vatican II. Lefebvre celebrated Mass only in the old Tridentine fashion. He found the principle of collegiality anathema. This archbishop continually ordained as priests solely candidates who shared his views.

The pope made a desperate attempt at reconciliation. 'Tell Monsignor Lefebvre of all my affliction, but also of all my affection,' he said. But he was adamant that Lefebvre submit to him, not vice versa. Repeatedly, Lefebvre's requests for audiences with the pope were refused.

The archbishop responded by establishing a seminary in Switzerland, which soon boasted over 100 students. Next Paul VI suspended the archbishop. Lefebvre responded by ordaining several priests, loyal to himself, and even consecrating four bishops. Eventually the two antagonists met. On 13 September 1976 Paul VI received Marcel Lefebvre at Castel Gandolfo, outside Rome. When Lefebvre advanced for a fraternal embrace, the pope drew back. The recalcitrant archbishop refused to recant and the two men parted in bitterness.

By now Paul VI was troubled with arthritis. Though he longed to make another visit to the New World, his doctors demurred. He remained in Rome, still active, occasionally contemplating resignation, always deciding against the idea. Increasingly, visitors to the Vatican noted his physical frailty. His eightieth birthday, on 26 September 1977, found him compiling Biblical texts about death. The following month, when terrorists downed a Lufthansa flight, killed its assistant pilot and threatened the lives of its passengers, the pope offered his own life in exchange for the freedom of the hostages. Inevitably, the gesture was ignored by the authorities, but it revealed the pope's increasing awareness that his life was drawing to its close.

One more blow was to afflict him. On 16 March 1978 his friend, the Christian Democrat leader, Aldo Moro, was kidnapped by the Red Brigade, his bodyguard gunned down. Moro's enemies resented his plans to form some coalition between the Christian Democrats and the Italian communists. They wanted the Italian government to release political prisoners.

Under threat of death, Moro remained a prisoner for fifty-five days, during which his friend the pope agonised and prayed for him. The Italian government refused to conclude a deal with the terrorists. Photographs of the terrified Moro were released. A letter from him reached the pope, pleading that the political prisoners be allowed to escape into exile and that Paul would use his influence to secure Moro's release.

In spite of the appeals of the Vatican, the Italian prime minister, Giulio Andreotti, refused to intervene. Paul VI resolved to appeal personally to Moro's captors. In a public letter he lauded Moro's virtues, recalling their student friendship, describing Moro as a son of the Church and a decent and honourable man. 'I beseech you to free Aldo Moro, simply and unconditionally,' wrote the pope, 'not because of my humble and well-meaning intercession but because he shares with you the common dignity of a human brother and because I dare hope that in all conscience you do not wish the cause of true human progress either to be stained with innocent blood or to be tortured by unnecessary suffering.' The pope even offered to ransom his old friend.

To no avail. On 9 May Moro's bullet-riddled corpse was found in Rome in the boot of a Renault hatchback. In a memorial service in the basilica of St John Lateran Pope Paul VI publicly lamented his death and reproached his killers.

Paul VI himself died on 6 August. Six days before his death he visited the tomb of an old friend, Cardinal Giuseppe Pizzardo, who had died at the age of ninety-three. The pope told the little crowd, 'We hope to meet him after death, which for us cannot be far away, in the glory of Our Lord Jesus Christ.'

Three days later he received an atheist at Castel Gandolfo, Sandro Petrini, the new socialist Italian head of state. Then an attack of cystitis began to make the pope's arthritis even more painful. On 6 August, the feast of the Transfiguration, in his bedroom the dying pope listened fitfully as the Mass for that day was celebrated. He received Holy Communion, both bread and wine, and then he suffered a savage heart attack. Paul VI began repeating the Lord's Prayer. At 9.41 he was dead.

Following tradition, Cardinal Jean Villot three times called him by his baptismal name, Giovanni. Then he announced, '*Vera papa mortuus.*'

CHAPTER EIGHT

John Paul I

After the conclave which elected John Paul I as pope, Cardinal Basil Hume, Archbishop of Westminster, declared that the new pope had been 'God's candidate.' God's candidate died thirty-three days later.

The mortal remains of Pope Paul VI, already decaying, had been laid to rest along with eighteen of his predecessors in the crypt of St Peter's, Rome, on 12 August 1978, six days after his death. A day later fifteen cardinals met in the Apostolic Palace, under the presidency of Cardinal Gonfalonieri (a man who, at eighty-five years old, clearly had little hope of becoming pope himself, even though Clement X was aged eighty when elected in 1670), to muse about Pope Paul's successor. Soon there were well over 100 cardinals in Rome. But the late pope still made his mark, having issued a decree that those aged eighty and over could not vote in a conclave electing a new pope. This excluded fifteen, leaving 111 men responsible for electing the new supreme pontiff. There would have been 112 had not the seventy-seven-year-old exiled Chinese Cardinal Paul Yu Pin not died during the conclave.

Because of the longevity of Pius XII and the brief pontificate of John XXIII, a mere eleven of these cardinals had ever before taken part in the election of a new pope. And a goodly number came from the third world.

But there was to be no third world pope elected in 1978. The Italian cardinals knew their task, none more than Archbishop Giovanni Benelli of Florence. To him only two persons seemed *papabili*, both of them Italians. One was the theologically right-of-centre Cardinal Giuseppe Siri of Genoa, the other the sixty-five-year-old Cardinal Albino Luciani, Patriarch of Venice. Luciani was his preferred candidate, a man born into the working classes yet opposed to communism; one who had moved to the right politically but still cared for the dispossessed; a distinguished churchman who opposed abortion and divorce. Equally crucially, this man was supported by Cardinal Gonfalonieri.

Another of Paul VI's reforms stipulated that at the most only twenty days should elapse between the death of a pope and the opening of a conclave to elect his successor. The cardinals allowed themselves nineteen days. Pope Paul had also changed the voting rules – incidentally pointing to the curious fashions and various ways in which the Catholic Church over the centuries has chosen the vicar of Christ. A new pope needed two-thirds of the votes of the cardinals (or two-thirds plus one if the assembled number was not exactly divisible by three). If no one was elected in this fashion, the new pontiff could be elected by a simple majority, plus one. Or else the names of two cardinals who had received most votes could be put to a ballot; or finally the cardinals might feel pleased to delegate the election to a smaller body, consisting of nine to fifteen of their members.

In 1978 there were four ballots. The third one indicated that the preferred candidate was Alberto Luciani. The fourth one gave him ninety votes. Thus elected, he announced that he would be called John Paul I. Twenty-four hours after the inauguration of the conclave, Cardinal Pericle Felice appeared on the balcony of St Peter's and declared, '*Annuntio vobis gaudium. Habemus papam*' ('I bring you news of great joy. We have a pope').

In choosing his name the new pope was honouring his predecessors: Pope John XXIII, who had consecrated him bishop in 1958, and Pope Paul VI, who had made him a cardinal in 1973. The curmudgeonly Cardinal Michel Lefebvre, who by his refusal to accept the reforms of the Second Vatican Council had already been a thorn in the side of Paul VI, now said he did not recognise the election since the over-eighties (including himself) had been excluded from voting. He added that the name John Paul I was a bad omen. His was the only sour note.

On his first address as pope from the balcony of St Peter's John Paul I humbly insisted that he had neither the heartfelt wisdom of Pope John nor the learning and culture of Pope Paul. Nonetheless, standing in their place he said he still hoped to serve the Church, and he asked for the prayers of the faithful. He also had no doubts about the importance of his new supreme office. As he had already written, 'If the laity, the priests, the members of religious orders and the bishops all stringently cling to the pope, no one can break up the Church.'

Yet despite this high view of his role, an extraordinary humility graced this pope. Bishops, he once wrote, vary. Some, like eagles, soar high above the world and carry important messages. Others, like nightingales, marvellously sing in praise of God. And others are miserable wrens, simply squawking on the lowest branch of the ecclesiastical tree. 'I am one of the last,' he said.

But this new pope did not despise his humble roots. As soon

as he was elected pope, Albino Luciani got in touch with his brother, Edoardo, his sister, Nina, and his nephews and nieces to let them know of this new, extraordinary development in his ecclesiastical career.

In origin, this was truly a man of the people. His family came from the Veneto. Luciani had been born on 17 October 1912 at Canale d'Agordo near Belluno. His mother was the second wife of a widower, who brought to the family two daughters from his first marriage. Albino was the first son of the second marriage, followed by Edoardo and then Nina. The family was not impoverished – but close to it. As he later wrote (in a letter addressed to Pinocchio!), 'a slice of bread with butter on both sides; a sweet with a soft centre; a sugar lump; at times even an egg or a pear – or even the skin of a pear: these were marvellous treats for the greedy and hungry boy you were; and so they were for me.'

Luciani's father had supported the family by working in the Murano glass factories and as a bricklayer and electrician, travelling to Germany and Switzerland to find work. He named Albino after a fellow workman who was killed in an accident at a German blast-furnace. Albino's sister married a bricklayer. Inevitably socialist ideas, some of them picked up by Albino's father, began to permeate the family, but none of these political ideas, at that time virtually anathema in the Catholic Church, prevented Albino's mother from remaining a devoutly practising Christian.

Both strands in his inheritance now influenced the future pope. To the end of his life, though resolutely opposed to Marxism, Luciani supported what he regarded as the legitimate aspirations of working men and women. Some strikes, he held, were undoubtedly justified. And, although they brought difficulties to many people who were not involved in them, the true response, he believed, was to accept the discomfort, not to complain, and to show solidarity with people fighting for their rights. This was, he wrote, 'pure Christian charity'. His father's social concerns seamlessly blended with his mother's piety.

Their son, Albino, was educated at the minor seminary of Feltre. This walled city, with its Renaissance houses and weather-worn steps, is renowned for the protection of the Blessed Virgin Mary, for on 11 July 1510, the citizens, attacked by the Imperial troops, barricaded themselves inside the cathedral and besought her help. The enemy soldiers found it impossible to smash down the cathedral doors. They set fire to the Duomo, but the flames did no damage. In vain they fired grenades at it. Finally, realising that they were up against Divine Intervention, they retired in dismay.

His next stage on the way to the priesthood was by way of the major seminary at Belluno, a city of arcaded streets and piazzas and an early sixteenth-century cathedral to which in 1743 was added a swaggering baroque campanile which rises for sixty-six metres. He studied under Alfredo Ottaviani, a noted anti-Protestant who would himself later be created cardinal, fulfilled his military service, and then went on to the Gregorian University in Rome. Then he returned home, as curate of the parish of Canale d'Agordo.

The future pope's career developed slowly. From curate he became a teacher at the seminary of Belluno. He prepared the way for the Eucharistic Congress of Belluno, which took place in 1949. Three years later his mother died, followed after two years by the death of his father. Then in December 1958 Pope John XXIII consecrated him Bishop of Vittório Véneto. Said the pope to the bishop, 'a good pastor is not just a man of learning or exquisite and abstruse language but rather one who is utterly available to God and to mankind.'

Luciani, in his fifty-sixth year, moved into the episcopal palace, the castle of San Martino at Ceneda, just outside Vittório Véneto, where his eighteenth-century cathedral boasted a thirteenth-century campanile and paintings in the sacristy by Tiepolo. He hadn't expected such a promotion. As he later wrote, as a theological student nobody taught him about being a cardinal, metropolitan and bishop, so he had to learn it from scratch. But learn he did. It seemed a reasonably quiet end to a peaceful clerical life.

Then his patron John XXIII called the Second Vatican Council. Albino Luciani never spoke at any session – though he did write documents about the Blessed Virgin Mary which were submitted to the Council. He also changed his mind. As the Council progressed, Luciani decided that Ottaviani had been wrong to so summarily dismiss Protestantism. Even in false opinions, he wrote, there can be a grain of truth. He also recognised the problems of the third world, and persuaded his diocese to link with a parish in Burundi.

Throughout his life Luciani remained sensitive to the needs of the third world. Rich Churches in the western world ought, he urged, to give 1 per cent of their income to poor Churches elsewhere. As a symbol, for these poorer Churches he donated a golden chain that had belonged to Pius XII and had been given to him by John XXIII on his ordination as bishop. He urged parish priests to devote the gifts of the faithful to the same cause. Aid to the third world certainly was continually raised, but, he observed, it was but a trifle. Far more was spent on armaments, while the people of the third world continued to suffer and die.

Cardinal Luciani was also acutely aware of the social problems in the so-called developed world. He particularly lamented the fact that many young people with university degrees and diplomas could not find jobs for themselves. There was also, he believed, a moral void in western society, noting that the quest for material advancement – to earn, to invest, to be surrounded with more and more creature comforts – meant that few believed their vocation ought to be simply to do good.

Eight years later Pope Paul VI appointed him as the forty-fifth Patriarch of Venice. Many workers from his former diocese had commuted there, to find menial jobs. Through them, Luciani claimed, he already knew his new diocese. He quoted his predecessor, Giuseppe Sarto: 'Though till now I have never seen you, yet already I bear you in my heart.' He reminded the mayor that the coins minted in Venice in AD 850 bore the slogan, 'Christ, save Venice', and promised that his own vow would be, 'Christ, bless Venice.'

Even now the patriarch remembered his humble origins. His new coat of arms bore three stars (symbolising faith, hope and charity), the lion of St Mark and then the mountains of Agordo. His motto was *Humilitas*. Yet he was far from willing to accept that the authority of the Church should be diminished, least of all the authority of the papacy. The synod of bishops, he insisted, was a mere consultative body. Jesus, he believed, had conferred authority first on the pope and, under him, on the bishops of the Church.

He was equally conservative – though leaving a way out for others of a liberal frame of mind – over Paul VI's encyclical *Humanae Vitae*. 'An individual's conscience must always be followed,' he said, adding, however, that 'the individual must have a well-formed conscience.' This future pope declared his belief both in preserving unspoilt the teachings of Christ and also in adapting them in the right way to modern times. There is some evidence that Luciani had written to Paul VI asking him not to condemn artificial contraception; but, once the encyclical was published, he remained loyal to his leader. As for abortion, he unreservedly condemned it, not only as a violation of the law of God but also as something that went against the deepest aspirations of women. Without giving chapter and verse for his opinion, he held that legalized abortions did not prevent clandestine 'back-street' abortions. But in this matter Pope John Paul I was simply agreeing with the Second Vatican Council, which had declared abortion to be the same as infanticide, and an 'abominable crime'.

This cardinal also warmed to the word with which Paul VI opened his Jubilee year: 'reconciliation' – reconciliation, as Luciani interpreted it, 'between ourselves and God, between ourselves and our fellow human beings on both the personal and the social level.' The cardinal spelled out some of the social problems where reconciliation was called for: power blocks against power blocks; nations against nations; parties against parties; individuals against other individuals – not to speak of aeroplane highjackings, bank robberies and the slaughter of innocent people by bombs. Those who reconciled themselves first with God could, he insisted, also renew their hearts, replacing hatred with love, anger with serenity and unbridled lust with moderate, healthy desires.

He also supported the pope's demand that men and women respond to hungry people who were dramatically calling to the rich, and reinforced the pope's concern at the anger of the poor, with its unforeseeable consequences. A third of the world, the cardinal pointed out, combined a remarkable abundance with shameless waste, whereas in two thirds of the world poverty steadily grew worse. As elsewhere in his writings and speeches, he touched on the obscenity of the money spent on armaments which could be used instead to raise the human family to a much higher economic, social and cultural level.

Yet in Venice Albino Luciani was frustrated. He preached in the cathedral of San Marco to hundreds of worshippers, but most of them (he lamented) were tourists who did not understand Italian. Then the editor of the journal *Messagero di Sant' Antonio* gave him a new outlet, by inviting the patriarch to write his amazing *Illustrissimi*.

This senior Italian prelate now revealed himself as a wondrously bizarre Patriarch of Venice. Luciani decided to write a series of letters to people he could never have met: for instance to Goethe; to one of the greatest of all Victorian novelists, Charles Dickens; to the Elizabethan playwright Christopher Marlowe; to the Italian poet Carducci; to G. K. Chesterton; to Mark Twain; to Sir Walter Scott; to St Teresa of Avila; to St Luke; and to Jesus himself.

'Dear Dickens,' he wrote, 'I'm a bishop who has been given the curious task of writing a letter once a month to some eminent person.' He decided to write first to Charles Dickens, since as a boy he had read his books and adored them, crammed as they were with love for the poor and a desire for social reform. The future pope empathised with the young Dickens, who had earned a living cleaning shoes, who had slept in an attic, whose father had been jailed for debt. For many of Dickens's contemporaries, escape from poverty came, Luciani noted, only from either drink or prostitution.

Instantly Luciani moved into *A Christmas Carol* and Scrooge. Brilliantly, the patriarch contrasted the position of Scrooge's miserable virtual slave, Bob Cratchit, with the situation of working people in twentieth-century Italy, buttressed by the trades union movement. Even so, he pointed out, there are still pockets of poverty and insecurity. Then Luciani turned to consider the problems of the third world. In the midst of all these problems, your principles still apply, he said to his 'dear

Dickens': love for the poor, not so much as individual persons as for whole peoples. Following the example of Jesus, he concluded, Christians were called upon to offer the poor whole-hearted love.

In his letter to Penelope, the wife of Ulysses, who had kept her suitors at bay during her husband's long absence, Luciani's wit – and his remarkable insight, as a celibate, into marriage – gleams in this letter. A husband, he muses, might delude himself into looking for a little 'distraction', arguing to himself that he won't go outside the fence but simply glance over the gate, to see what goes on outside. Both husband and wife have to put up with monotony, Luciani continues. Then either Venus or Adonis turns up, often in the form of an office colleague, offering apparently more mutual interests than the spouse. The journalist patriarch discovered a lovely quote from the seventeenth-century Jesuit St Francis de Sales about this: 'married couples who are saints exchange many caresses.' Finally, he recognised that even the best of couples can sometimes become bad-tempered. 'If such times can't be avoided,' Luciani counselled, 'spouses should take it in turns to be ill-tempered.'

Luciani was shrewd. He told Figaro, the barber of Seville, about the Beatles. Their music, he said, was considered young people's music; but what it did was make money for canny old men.

Cardinal Luciani was no puritan. Beauty, he insisted, is one of God's gifts. To dress with elegance and taste is something to be praised, especially in women. Even cosmetics, he wrote in his *Illustrissimi*, are not in many cases something to disapprove of. But the same passage reveals that he always saw deeper than the passing show. These earthly goods, he wrote, are all evanescent. To be a friend of God, to be close to him in a good life and to be sincere in religion are far more secure and lasting.

This prelate was endlessly inventive in devising the recipients of his letters. He wrote to a saintly bear, who had eaten St Romedio's horse, repented and thenceforth carried the saint around; he wrote to Mr Pickwick ('a dying reader would be justified in asking God to grant him a further ten days of life to finish the last instalment of the book that immortalises you'); he wrote to Sir Walter Scott ('your books exalt goodness and loyalty, and can be put into the hands of children'); and he wrote to Pinocchio, advising him on his choice of girlfriends.

Illustrissimi is filled with jokes. Read it to discover the different ways in which an Englishman, a Frenchman, an Italian, a German, a Dane and an Eskimo react on being served a glass of beer with a fly in it. Pope John Paul I relished St Teresa of Avila in part because she often smiled and could make others laugh. He could make jokes against himself. 'Never have I been beaten by persecutors,' he once wrote, adding ruefully, 'but many people have upset me by shouting in the street, having their television sets on too loud or making slurping noises as they eat their soup.'

Cardinal Luciani emphatically agreed with St Teresa of Avila's view that a sad saint is a poor saint. Luciani invented a tale of an Irishman sitting at the gate of heaven and wondering whether he would be let in, since he had never given food to the hungry nor visited the sick nor those in prison. When his turn came to be admitted or rejected, Christ said to him, 'You did do something. You told me some jokes, made me laugh and cheered me up. Off you go to heaven.' For Luciani a jest could be a work of holiness.

For this pope a jest always had a spiritual undertow. In his reading he came across Jonathan Swift, who had a servant who did not wish to clean Swift's boots, on the grounds that they would surely become dusty again. The next morning Swift asked his servant to get his horses and carriage ready without having any breakfast, on the grounds that the servant would soon become hungry again. As Luciano concluded, many Catholics in his day were unwilling to confess their sins, arguing that soon they would sin again. But, he said, to keep oneself clean in the meantime cannot be a bad idea.

What did he write to Jesus? The first sentence of his letter reads, 'I've been criticised.' Then, strangely, he began to eulogise Jesus's intelligence, a feature not at all emphasised in the Gospels. During his life on earth Jesus did not have the intelligence of God. Theologically speaking, this is usually explained by the doctrine of *kenosis*. The word is derived from the Greek verb 'to empty', and the doctrine is classically expressed by St Paul in his letter to the Philippians, which declares that, 'being in the form of God, Jesus counted it not a prize to be on an equality with God, but emptied himself, taking the form of a servant, being made in the likeness of men.' Next, Luciani begs forgiveness for finding two of Jesus's beatitudes almost impossible to accept: blessed are the poor and blessed are those who are persecuted. Most people want riches and comfort, wrote Luciani. Would it not be possible for Jesus to change the subject? Audaciously, the cardinal was jesting with his Saviour.

But, of course, Luciani also worshipped Jesus. He added that men raised Jesus on a cross and from there his outstretched arms drew countless people to him. What a light of intelligence flowed from his teaching, declared Luciani. Jesus sought not his own glory, wrote Luciani, but simply to obey his heavenly Father. Albino Luciani asked his readers to judge, was this God or merely a great and good man?

Cardinal Luciani felt that this letter was the worst of all that he had penned to the men and women of the past. This devout, humorous, humble follower of Jesus confessed, 'I have never been so dissatisfied with what I have just written.' He had, he declared, expressed badly what could have been written much better. But what truly mattered, according to Albino Luciani, was not what anyone wrote about the Christ but that many should love and imitate him.

On the morning after his election, this merry pope Gianpaolo (as he was already affectionately being called) celebrated Mass for his cardinals. In his homily he touched on the dangers faced by the world, from mankind's ecological greed and from the threat of nuclear warfare. He also promised to press on indomitably with the renewal promised by the Second Vatican Council.

Next, he declared his intention to work for the reunion of Christendom – adding, however, 'without diluting doctrine.' This pope would soon speak not of heretics but of Christian brethren who were not fully in communion with him. Finally, he promised to work with all those, Christian or not, who sincerely wished to enter into dialogue with the Catholic Church for the sake of peace.

Journalists warmed to this papal journalist. On 1 September he addressed eight hundred of them, and most of them were charmed by his speech. One of them (the Irishman T. P. O'Mahoney) went so far as to declare that 'with his election the papacy and therefore the Church could well be on the threshold of a new and exciting era, an era of spiritual renewal, intensified social concern and fresh ecumenical endeavours.' Two days later, on the feast of St Gregory the Great, his ministry was inaugurated. Observers noted a major change: John Paul I refused to be crowned with the papal tiara; he refused to be enthroned; he was simply declared supreme pastor of the Church – for that was enough.

He already knew the tensions faced by a leader of the Catholic Church, let alone the pope. He once recalled that at the battle of Poitiers in 1356 the King of France was fighting beside his son, who, watching over his father, would shout, 'Father, look to the right! Father, look to the left!' That, declared Luciani while still Patriarch of Venice, is what he always had to do. Every time an old rite is abandoned people on the right shout 'impiety' and 'sacrilege'. By contrast, those on the left would blithely, even merrily, dismantle everything, calling for the new simply for the sake of newness, seeing idolatry and superstition everywhere, even going so far as to assert that for the sake of God's dignity it might be better not to mention God at all. Luciani's passion in denouncing the left perhaps indicates that by now he leaned more to the right. But, he added, 'it is hard going'.

As a member of the Church's hierarchy, he knew where his duties lay. He accepted that charismatic Christian leaders were necessary for the Church – acting as accelerators who promoted progress and renewal. But the hierarchy also had a role, as a brake, speaking for prudence and stability. And the hierarchy must in the end rule over the charismatics.

He also set his face against the ordination of women to the priesthood. 'Women don't rule in the Church,' declared Pope John Paul I (in an address about the redoubtable St Teresa of Avila). 'That is a function of the hierarchy.' But, the pope added, 'very often women aspire, promote and at times even direct.' He went so far as to concede that women are much more sensitive to religion than men. They are, this pope declared, far more capable than men of giving themselves to great causes.

This was a pope who knew his own mind. Luciani had harsh words to say both about capitalism and about Marxism. He did not doubt the former promoted industrial development and defended personal freedom, but it had also in the previous century caused enormous suffering to the poor and still created great inequalities. Competition could readily degenerate into a ferocious, pitiless struggle. As for Marxism, it had alerted many people to the sufferings of the working classes and insisted on the duty of solidarity, but it had also crushed personal freedom and swept away religious values.

Luciani believed that capitalism could be – indeed must be – profoundly changed. Marxism he was less sure about. Could it be redeemed? He quoted his mentor, Paul VI, that it would be a dangerous illusion to accept any Marxist analysis of society in the hope of separating this from the atheistic ideology which it also promulgated. Yet the cardinal acknowledged the value of Paul VI's determination, in his quest for the peace of the world, to mediate with atheistic communists as well as supposedly Christian capitalist countries.

But death was in the air. One evening, shortly after Albino Luciani accepted the mantle of St Peter, Metropolitan Nikodim, the Patriarch of Leningrad, died in the pope's own study. Six days later, at 5.30 a.m. on 29 September 1978, the pope himself was found dead. By his bedside was *The Imitation of Christ* by Thomas à Kempis. His light was still on. A doctor certified that he must have died of a massive heart attack around 11 p.m. the previous evening.

Inevitably, conspiracy theories about his death abounded. After all, an attempt had been made on the life of his predecessor. Who could hate Luciani enough to murder him? Perhaps, it was suggested, he was poisoned because he planned to attack corruption in the Vatican Bank. On the other hand, maybe he was intending to attack freemasonry, and therefore powerful Italian freemasons killed him. Thirdly, it was possible that he planned to dismiss intransigent members of the curia (as one commentator observed, at the time of his appointment, the curia was still set in granite). Maybe, therefore, members of the curia did away with the new pope. Finally, was he killed because of his supposed intention to cancel *Humanae Vitae*?

Not one of these suppositions was supported by any concrete evidence. But his predecessor had been subject to an assassination attempt. His successor John Paul II, would be the victim of an assassin's bullets, and on a visit to Sarajevo in 1997, his motorcade would narrowly escape an attempt to blow it up. It would have been wise to commission an autopsy of the pope's corpse, if only finally to dismiss them. No autopsy was carried out.

After John Paul I's death, Basil Hume, Cardinal Archbishop of Westminster, summed up Pope Albino Luciani as 'a man rooted in the Gospel, but with his feet firmly on twentieth-century ground and with his eyes twinkling as he calmly surveyed the contemporary, tempestuous, troubled world, smiling at its absurdities, regretting its evil, rejoicing in its good.' Basil Hume went on to affirm that this was a consummate teacher, widely read, a born raconteur with a fund of anecdotes and illustrations at his command, a man who understood people from within, who identified with them, yet a man to whom his faith was the breath of life and the source of joy.

CHAPTER NINE

John Paul II

So a new conclave opened, called as soon as possible for 14 October, in part because many cardinals had other work to do in far-away dioceses as well as to participate in the crucial work of electing a pope. Ninety-five cardinals reached Rome for John Paul I's Requiem Mass. Another sixteen hurried to the eternal city where, when the conclave began, altogether 111 were assembled – exactly the same number as in the previous conclave that had elected John Paul I.

The death of the pope had stunned many of them. In preaching about him, the Cardinal Archbishop of Genoa, Giuseppe Siri, had tried to dispel these gloomy thoughts. Cardinal Siri listed some of the themes set out by John Paul I: fidelity to Catholic doctrine, to Church discipline and to spirituality. Then, Siri declared, the fugitive pope, having opened a new era in the Catholic Church, had quietly gone away. Siri declined to reveal who, he thought, would further this new era. Maybe, Siri undoubtedly mused and hinted, that person was himself.

Meanwhile Karol Wojtyla was in the Franciscan monastery of

Kalwaria, saying a Mass for the dead pope. Then he set off for Rome, his parting words, 'My friends, pray for me.'

On Monday 16 October the laity and religious assembled in St Peter's Square learned that the new pope was to be neither Siri nor any other Italian cardinal. On the eighth ballot, the successor to John Paul I was elected with over ninety votes. Just after a quarter past seven in the evening Cardinal Pericle Felice appeared on the balcony of the basilica of St Peter and proclaimed '*Habemus papam.*' The new pope, he told the crowd, had taken the name John Paul II. When, slowly, this Polish pope advanced to the balcony, the crowd welcomed the handsome, fifty-eight-year-old Cardinal Karol Wojtyla, Archbishop of Krakow, the first non-Italian pope for 455 years. Wojtyla made his entrance theatrically; after all, in his youth he had been an actor.

Those assembled in St Peter's Square also gained their first taste of a Polish pontiff. Italian Catholics, as all Catholics, honour the Blessed Virgin Mary, but none more so than Polish Catholics. Our Lady, Polish Catholics hold, is the Queen of Poland, a belief constantly reiterated in the face of the communist rulers of their nation. In his inaugural speech on his election as pope, John Paul II quoted the Polish poet Mieczytlaw Kotlarcyk about the Holy Maiden who guarded the Polish shrine of Czestochowa. And now from the central balcony of St Peter's, John Paul II told those present in the square that he accepted this call not only in obedience to Jesus but also 'in utter faithfulness to Mary, the Mother of Christ and of the Church.'

Two weeks after his election, John Paul II was at Mentorella, some thirty kilometres from Rome, to venerate a twelfth-century statue of the Blessed Virgin which is cherished by a group of Polish monks. When on 19 September 1979 he arrived in Dublin airport on his pilgrimage to the republic of Ireland, in invoking God's blessing on that land he added, 'I commend all her people to the prayers of our Blessed Lady, Mary, Mother of Jesus and Queen of Peace, under whose patronage I place my pastoral visit.'

At his inaugural Mass as pope, celebrated in the Sistine Chapel beneath Michelangelo's fresco of the harrowing of hell, John Paul II declared that, although he was a son of Poland, from that day he also became a Roman. But Poland had formed and nurtured him. His papal coat of arms retains much of the heraldry of that of the Bishop of Krakow, with in its right-hand corner, the letter M for Mary. And on his election he generously declared that there would have been no Polish pope on the throne of St Peter but for the fortitude and heroic hope of Cardinal Wyszynski, who had feared neither prison nor suffering.

Born on 18 May 1920, thirty kilometres south-west of Krakow in Wadowice, Wojtyla was the son of a retired army lieutenant. The future pope's mother, Emilia Kaxzorouwska, came from Silesia, a part of Poland occupied by the Austrians. A schoolteacher, she died three years after his birth, aged only forty-five, while giving birth to a still-born girl. Four years later Karol's elder brother, Edmund, also died, after catching scarlet fever in the hospital where he was training as a doctor.

Their country was not entirely at unity with itself. Although most of its citizens were Catholics, to the east lived a substantial number of Orthodox Christians, to the west lived Lutherans and a tenth of the population was Jewish.

Young Karol attended the local school from the age of seven, moving to the local high school four years later. As well as shining academically and enthusiastically participating in school plays, he also exulted in games: football, canoeing, swimming and above all skiing. He also served as an altar boy in the parish church of Wadowice.

In 1938 he and his father moved to Krakow, a city of Renaissance houses, its cathedral rising alongside its castle, the whole set on a bend of the River Vistula. Here Karol entered the Jagiellonian University to study Polish language and literature. As an undergraduate he loved not only poetry but also theatre, and ventured into student acting.

When Poland was overrun by the Nazis and divided between Germany and Soviet Russia, such cultural activities could survive only underground. The future pope worked in a stone quarry, promoted to shot-firer who placed the cartridges that dynamited the rocks, and then in a chemical factory. In these humble tasks he learned a lot. As he later wrote, 'Work is something that distinguishes human beings from the rest of creation.' He even wrote a poem called *The Quarry*, declaring in it that men mature through physical work, when their hands have been split into ravines. But he also continued to study and to act, taking the risk of performing in Polish nationalist plays proscribed by the Nazis.

With friends he had formed a theatre group, Studio 39, as early as 1939, a group which transformed itself in 1941 into the Rhapsodic Theatre. Their aim was to keep alive Polish literature in the face of Nazi hostility.

In 1941, when Wojtyla was only twenty-one, his father died; but Karol found a new spiritual father, the Cardinal Archbishop of Krakow, Adam Sapieha, who gave sanctuary in his episcopal palace to Wojtyla and a few other students. The archbishop arranged for his protégé's papers to be 'lost' by the Polish boss of the chemical factory, so that the German authorities would not be able to find the student.

When the Russians liberated Poland in January 1945, Wojtyla was free to return to the Jagiellonian University. He graduated in August of the following year. At the age of twenty-six he was ordained priest, on All Saints' Day 1946. The following morning, on 2 November, his first Mass was celebrated in a chapel of Krakow cathedral. Then he returned to Wadowice, where he celebrated three Masses – one for his mother, the second for his father, the third for his brother – in the exquisite baroque parish church of Our Lady.

The war was over, but the Soviets now controlled Poland. Yet this did not prevent the newly-ordained priest from studying for a couple of years in Rome, at the Angelicum University. His Austrian mother had made sure that the family spoke German as well as Polish. Living in the Belgian College at Rome, Wojtyla now added French to his linguistic skills. In Rome, too, he perfected his grasp of Italian. And, as a would-be poet and dramatist, he composed there a thesis on the writings of the Spanish mystic and poet St John of the Cross under the tuition of a distinguished Dominican scholar Fr. Réginald Garrigou-Lagrange. It was accepted *summa cum laude*, and Karol was awarded the degree of Doctor of Divinity.

He spent his holidays working for Polish refugees in Belgium, Holland and France. Then he returned to Poland, to work as a curate in Polish churches. He spent a year in the parish of Niegowic, near Krakow. Then his superiors moved him to the church of St Florian, in Krakow itself. He attracted parishioners not only by his eloquence in the pulpit but also because he loved playing football with their sons. He would take young members of his parish on hiking trips, carrying along a portable altar to celebrate Mass in the open air.

Soon this man was recognised as one of Poland's promising ecclesiastical scholars. His parish released him to work at the

Catholic University of Lublin. He began to teach social ethics to priests at the Krakow seminary. Eventually the university recognised his scholarship by appointing him professor of moral philosophy.

Yet these were not easy years for Catholics in Soviet-controlled Poland. In September 1953 Cardinal Stefan Wyszinski was confined to house arrest in a monastery. Soon eight Polish bishops, some nine hundred priests and more than two thousand Catholic laymen and women had been arrested and confined to gaols.

In these turbulent years, Wojtyla was made auxiliary Bishop of Krakow (he was on a canoeing holiday with students when the news came). He was thirty-eight years old. On his episcopal seal he had inscribed the words '*Totus Tuus*' (All yours). Eight years later, in 1964 and aged forty-three, he was elevated: consecrated Archbishop of Krakow. He was, incidentally, the first man born in the working classes to have been so elevated. (His protector during the war, Cardinal Sapieha, being of noble birth, also rejoiced in the name Prince Adam Stefan Sapieha-Kodenski, and some of the faithful called him Prince-Prince Sapieha, since he was both a worldly prince and a prince of the Church!) In 1967 Paul VI made him a cardinal. Sapieha was a Polish patriot and a master of the courageous gesture. He refused to don the robes of a cardinal until his country was liberated. Thus he never wore them.

Wojtyla relished contact with the young. One of his poems declares that, in confirming children, his hand senses their trust. Wojtyla was also already a man who had appeared on the international stage of the Second Vatican Council, speaking twice at its opening sessions, in 1962 and 1963. In these speeches, in marked contrast to his later behaviour as pope, Wojtyla seemed a radical. He quoted St John of the Cross not on the certainty of faith but on the 'mystery', even the 'darkness' of faith.

When in March 1975, at the request of Pope Paul VI, Karol Wojtyla conducted the retreat of the curia, Wojtyla quoted St John of the Cross:

> To attain to that which you do not know,
> you must also pass through that which you do not know.
> To attain to that which you do not possess,
> you must pass through that which you do not possess.
> To reach that which you are not,
> You must pass through that which you are not.

In October 1963 this man, one of the most authoritarian of twentieth-century popes, condemned authoritarianism. He counselled the assembled bishops to proclaim the rights not only of other Christian bodies but also of unbelievers. He stressed the need not for a monologue from the Church to the world but for dialogue.

Even when elected pope, he still insisted that his mission was to continue the reforms of the Second Vatican Council and that 'collegiality', pluralism and ecumenicism would have prime importance in his work. This was scarcely to be so.

For his years Wojtyla was an exceedingly fit man. Annually he would take a skiing holiday at Zakopane. He was also an enthusiastic traveller – a trait even more developed when he became pope. But at this time Poland was both his base and his strength. Such was the power of Catholicism there that in 1977 the Polish premier, Edward Gierek, felt it judicious to visit Rome and be received by Pope Paul VI himself.

Meanwhile the future pope had already been travelling. He

reached Canada and the United States in 1969. In 1973 he was at a Eucharistic Congress in Melbourne, Australia. Three years later he was at another Eucharistic Congress in Philadelphia, where he obliquely criticised the government of his homeland by speaking of the Polish people's hunger for freedom and justice. He and Wyszynski were in West Germany the following year.

These trips clearly gave the future pope a taste for more travel. Latin America was the first part of the world visited by John Paul II after his election. The Latin American bishops were to meet at Puebla, Mexico, on 27 January 1979. With a brief stop-over in the Dominican Republic, the pope arrived in Mexico City on the day the bishops' conference convened. Millions cheered as his motorcade sped to Puebla. His speech there condemned those who argued that the Christian gospel allied itself with revolutionary social change; but on the same visit he also condemned those whose greed had consigned many Indians to poverty.

His devotion to the Blessed Virgin was also evident, for at Guadalupe is an image of Mary based on her alleged appearance to an Indian, speaking to him in his own language, in 1531. The pope prayed to her. Some were saddened that the pope did not speak of social justice. Others regretted his stance that the Church should eschew political alliances, especially those with the left. Most were overjoyed to see him. And he did speak of workers' rights. He did offer himself as the voice of those unable to speak for themselves. He did defend the legitimacy of workers' organisatons. He did support the demand for a fairer distribution of the country's goods.

Then he visited Poland, the first pope ever to enter a country ruled by communists. Inevitably, he visited the shrine of the Black Virgin at Czestochowa. He came to Krakow, to Gniezno, to Wadowice where he was born, to infamous Oswiecim, to Warsaw. Two million Poles waited for him in that city. At Czestochowa he spoke out for human rights, particularly insisting that the State must ensure the rights of the Church.

At Oswiecim he said prayers in the cell where Fr. Maximilian Kolbe had been murdered by the Nazis. Here, between the railway lines that had served trains bringing millions to their deaths in the gas chambers, the pope celebrated Mass. Two former inmates were there, dressed in their striped concentration-camp costume. The cross on the altar was wreathed in barbed wire. The pope spoke of the inalienable dignity and rights of human beings. He remembered the Jews, who had brought to humankind the commandment, 'Thou shalt not kill' and then, as he put it, experienced to the full what killing means.

Then in Krakow he proclaimed that he was a pope who had no fear of the workers – they had always, he said, been particularly close to his heart. Yet he was no longer a radical. He took to attacking what he called the moral sickness afflicting young people, becoming more and more conservative in his utterances, modifying what many regarded as his reactionary talks by also denouncing what he called 'consumerism'.

Yet he remained extraordinarily charismatic. In Ireland he celebrated a mass for young people at Galway. His homily ended, 'Young people of Ireland, I love you! Young people of Ireland, I bless you! I bless you in the name of our Lord Jesus Christ.' After the words, 'Young people of Ireland, I love you,' the pope was interrupted by twelve minutes of ecstatic cheering.

In Ireland too, 'on my knees', he begged those who wished to kill each other to turn away from violence. He attempted to reinforce these words by appealing to the witness of a famous Irish Catholic and martyr. The pope remembered that in 1975, as Cardinal Archbishop of Krakow, he had assisted at the canonisation of St Oliver Plunkett, who for twelve years had been primate of all Ireland. 'As bishop he preached a message of pardon and peace,' the pope reminded his hearers. 'He was indeed a defender of the oppressed and the advocate of justice, but he would never condone violence. There was no rancour in his heart, even when he died,' declared John Paul II. 'His dying words were words of forgiveness for all his enemies.'

The pope's attempt at reconciling the people of strife-torn Northern Ireland led him to observe how moved he was that his invitation to that country by its leading Catholics had been taken up by representatives of the Church of Ireland and by leaders and members of other Churches, including Northern Irish ones. These invitations indicated to him that the Second Vatican Council was achieving its work; that he was meeting with his fellow-Christians as people who together confessed Jesus as Lord and who were drawing closer together as they sought for unity and common witness.

He quoted Jesus: 'Those who live by the sword will perish by the sword.' No solution could come by way of terrorism and the murder of defenceless people; peace could never flourish in a climate of intimidation and death, of recrimination and retaliation. And no Irish Protestant, he affirmed, should regard the pope as in any way an enemy, a danger or a threat. 'My desire is that instead Protestants would see in me a friend and a brother in Christ.'

Then he insisted that the tragic events taking place in Northern Ireland did not arise from religious divisions.

> Despite what is so often repeated before world opinion, this is not a religious war, a struggle between Catholics and Protestants. On the contrary, Catholics and Protestants, as people who confess Christ, taking inspiration from their

> faith and the Gospel, are seeking to draw closer to one another in unity and peace. When they recall the greatest commandment of Jesus, they cannot behave otherwise.

From Ireland he flew to the United States of America, answering an invitation to address the general assembly of the United Nations Organisation. The days had long passed since twentieth-century popes had distrusted such international means towards peace. Now the Holy See had a permanent observer to the UN, and John Paul II's predecessor, Paul VI, had already addressed the members of the organisation.

In his address of 2 October 1979 the pope praised the UN's commitment to peaceful coexistence and collaboration between the nations of the world, which was of course a necessary platitude. Then he spelled out in detail his own visions and anxieties. He enumerated what he believed to be the essential rights of human beings: to life, liberty and security; to food, clothing, housing, health-care, rest and leisure; to freedom of expression, education and culture; to freedom of thought, conscience and religion; to choose a state of life, found a family and enjoy all the conditions necessary for family life; to property, work, adequate working conditions and a just wage; to freedom of movement; to nationality and residence; to political participation and the right to take part in the free choice of the political system to which one belongs.

But, the pope added, material goods by their very nature provoke divisions and conflict. He deplored the frightful disparities between the excessively rich and the majority – the poor, sometimes even destitute, lacking food, condemned to hunger and disease. Without a concern for spiritual matters, modern civilisation was prey to such systematic threats against human life and well-being.

He finally warned against the armaments race. 'The ancients said: *Si vis pacem, para bellum.* But can our age still really believe that the breathtaking spiral of armaments is at the service of world peace? In alleging the threat of a potential enemy, is it really not rather the intention to keep for oneself a means of threat, in order to get the upper hand with the aid of one's own arsenal of destruction?'

As one of his acute but uncritical admirers, the British Catholic convert Lord Longford, remarked, the pope won the hearts of thousands of Ukrainian and Spanish immigrants in Philadelphia. (He reminded the Ukrainians that Pope Paul VI had given a stone from the tomb of St Peter to be incorporated into the stones of their cathedral.) He was, says the same witness, received with almost delirious applause in Chicago. In Washington he addressed five thousand nuns at the national shrine of the Immaculate Conception. (Some of them were displeased that he here reiterated his opposition to the ordination of women.)

A visit to Turkey, a predominantly Muslim country, forced John Paul II to reconsider the papal attitude to other ways of approaching God. Here security was tight. A young man, Mehmet Ali Agca, who had been imprisoned for killing the editor of a Turkish newspaper, had escaped from gaol. Moreover, he had written to that same newspaper that his only reason for escaping from prison was to murder the pope.

In that same year the pope had also visited France, once the cradle of Catholicism but now resolutely agnostic, and he made a thirteen-day visit to Brazil, where he spoke movingly of the evils of under-nourishment and unjust social conditions.

In 1980 he was in Germany, the home of the Reformation, in order to celebrate the seven hundredth anniversary of the death of Albertus Magnus, the brilliant medieval scholar who had been canonised in 1932. This was yet another lightning visit, taking in Cologne, where Albertus Magnus had died, Mainz, where the pope met representatives of the German Protestant churches, and Munich, the heart of German Catholicism.

Germany was also a hot-bed of new thinking, spearheaded by Hans Küng, Professor of Catholic Theology at the University of Tübingen. Hans Küng much disliked what he considered the pope's reactionary views, and told him so in an article published in several major European journals. John Paul II responded by depriving the professor of his status as an accredited Catholic theologian.

No university can deserve the rightful esteem of the world of learning unless it excels in seriousness and therefore in freedom of investigation, the pope proclaimed. But in this same speech (given to the president of US Catholic universities in 1979) he took back part of his proclamation with the remark, 'It behoves the theologian to be free, but with the freedom that is openness to the truth and light that comes from faith and fidelity to the Church.'

One of Wojtyla's poems, written during the Second Vatican Council, addresses St Peter himself:

> Peter, you are the ground.
> Others walk over you,
> Not clear to where they are bound.
> You guide their steps.

Pius X once said that 'the multitudes of the faithful have no other duty than to let themselves be led and as a docile flock to follow their shepherds.' John Paul II clearly seemed to share the same view.

Yet in attacking Hans Küng, for once this immensely intelligent, remarkably self-confident pope had met his match. Belatedly he discovered that the university of Tübingen is not at all subservient to the Vatican. Professor Hans Küng was confirmed in his post by the university authorities, and the pope retired from the fray, powerless.

Towards the end of that year he made sure that his own views prevailed during a month-long synod of bishops called to discuss the role of the family in the late twentieth-century world. Some of the assembled hierarchy wanted John Paul II to soften the condemnation of artificial birth control made in Paul VI's 1968 encyclical *Humanae Vitae*. John Paul II refused to do so. Inevitably the pope also condemned abortion, arguing that 'the defence of the absolute inviolability of unborn life is part of the defence of human rights and human dignity.'

Those bishops who pleaded that divorced Catholics might still receive the sacrament of Holy Communion were likewise disappointed by the pope's response. John Paul II believed that, 'The very possibility of divorce in the sphere of civil law makes stable and permanent marriages more difficult for everyone.'

At the beginning of 1981 he was on his travels again. In twelve days he visited Karachi, Japan and the Philippines. In Karachi he reminded his hearers that Abraham was the father not only of Jews and Christians but also of Muslims. In Manila he annoyed some members of the Catholic clergy by warning them to stay out of politics, while he himself spoke politically by, for instance, insisting that governments safeguard human rights. In Japan he said Masses both at Hiroshima and Nagasaki, the only cities to have suffered devastation by atomic bombs.

His next plans for foreign travel included a visit to Switzerland in June. But popes are too prominent not to attract the attention of dangerous fanatics and Paul VI had been the victim of a failed assassination attempt. Writing in 1979, two of John

Paul II's biographers commented on his disregard for his own safety. One described the pope's visit to an old friend in Rome's Gemelli hospital: 'He travelled in an open car and was cheered along the route. Despite the problems created for the security forces, he would not be content to remain "the prisoner of the Vatican".' The other commented, 'The pope's habit of plunging into the crowd whenever he felt like it gave his security men nightmares.' Their fears were to prove well-founded.

On 13 May his open-topped jeep was circling the crowd in the square of St Peter's as he blessed and waved to the people. Amongst the crowd was Mehmet Ali Agca. Amazingly enough, the Turkish government had already told the security forces that Agca had succeeded in entering Italy on a forged passport. At nineteen minutes past five, shots rang out, and the pope fell down, clutching his chest. He had been hit by three bullets. Agca's shots also wounded two women who were in the crowd close to the pope.

The white papal jeep sped into the Vatican and an ambulance took the pope to the Gemelli hospital. Although the last rites were administered, Pope John Paul II survived a five-hour operation. Agca was apprehended and sentenced to life imprisonment. Many speculated that perhaps the Soviets were behind the attempted assassination of a man who so consistently was undermining their hold on the Catholic countries of the eastern bloc, particularly in the case of his native Poland. But no proof was forthcoming to back up this speculation.

A year later, on the anniversary of the assassination attempt, the pope flew to Fatima, to thank the Virgin Mary for saving his life. 'One hand fired the gun,' he told a huge crowd; 'another hand guided the bullet.' Then, ever the master of theatre, he placed Agca's bullet in the crown of two thousand diamonds that encircles the head of the statue of the Madonna.

Nor did the assassination attempt blunt his outspokenness over Poland. While John Paul II was spending nineteen days in hospital, Cardinal Stefan Wyszynski died. The pope's first Sunday address after he left the Gemelli hospital declared that Wyszynski had been the keystone which had held together the Polish Church. He was speaking in praise of a prince of the Church who had frequently accused the Polish communist government of bad faith in its relationships with Catholicism. As a result, in 1953, he had been placed under arrest.

In June 1981 John Paul II had suffered a brief relapse after the assassination attempt. For six months the pope took life more easily, though he still welcomed the faithful at Castel Gandolfo. Fortunately, too, the previously agile pontiff had commissioned a swimming pool for his summer palace, and would happily splash around in it, making the sign of the cross before he took the plunge. But since that time his health gradually deteriorated. An operation on the colon was followed by another in 1996 to remove his appendix, the sixth operation he had undergone since his election.

No longer could he flamboyantly kiss the ground whenever he arrived in a far country by plane. Now a bowl with some of the earth was lifted to his lips. When he tried to make his 1995 Christmas broadcast he slowed down and finally stopped, retiring to his apartments inside the Vatican. His left hand at times began to shake uncontrollably. On his visit to Latin America in February 1996 at the age of seventy-five (his sixty-ninth trip since his election, and one made against the advice of his doctors) John Paul II was visibly suffering. When he reached Hungary in September of the same year, again he was unable to finish a major speech (at the Benedictine monastery of Pannonhalma).

Vatican observers began to speculate on his successor, with

many suggesting he might be Cardinal Carlo Maria Martini of Milan, some nominating Cardinal Vinko Puljic of Vrhbosna-Sarajevo and others pointing to a possible third world pope – perhaps Cardinal Frances Arinze of Nigeria.

The reigning pope had other ideas. The morning after his election as pope, John Paul II had asked the assembled cardinals, 'What is the fate that the Lord has in store for his Church in the coming years and what path will humanity take as it draws near to the year 2000?' He began to plan a splendid ecumenical celebration in the Holy Land for the millennium.

And though physically weak, his views remained as uncompromisingly robust as ever. In 1995 he issued a 150-page document, *Ecclesia in Africa*, laying some of the blame for misery, war and instability in Africa – the poorest continent in the world – on the 'dishonesty of corrupt government leaders', who had diverted public funds to themselves. 'Whatever the legal camouflage may be, this is plain theft,' the pope continued.

Published while he was on a visit to Cameroon, South Africa and Kenya, his statement called on the Church to be 'the voice of the voiceless', and on local bishops' conferences to establish justice and peace commissions that would monitor human rights. In issuing this, in parts scathing, document, John Paul II was acting out what many of his Church considered to be the true role of a pope, for this was not something that took by surprise the leaders of the 100 million African Catholics. He seemed to be accepting collegiality. The previous year a synod of African bishops had met at the Vatican to discuss their problems: not only that of oppressive, authoritarian regimes, but also those concerning relations with Islam and how the African Church could lose its Eurocentric bias and respond to the values and cultures of Africa itself.

Not all of these initiatives were peculiar to John Paul II. In his encyclical *Mater et magistra* John XXIII had argued that it was impossible for the wealthy nations to look with indifference on the hunger, misery and poverty of those nations whose citizens did not enjoy even the most elementary human rights. There could be no lasting peace, he said, as long as such glaring economic and social inequalities persisted.

As for the papal thrust to de-Europeanise Catholicism on other continents, as early as the pontificate of Pius XI, Chinese and Japanese bishops had been consecrated – six Chinese in 1926, the first Japanese bishop of Nagasaki in 1927. Native bishops of South-east Asia and India were consecrated in 1933. When Pius XI became pope native priests numbered no more than 2,670. When he died they numbered over 7,000; and forty mission dioceses were under the supervision of native bishops.

In *Ecclesia in Africa* the Holy Father was articulating the concerns and the endeavours of native bishops. 'In many parts of Africa the winds of change are blowing strongly. Even more insistently people are demanding the recognition and promotion of human rights and freedoms,' he observed, adding, 'I note with satisfaction that the Church in Africa, faithful to its vocation, stands resolutely on the side of the oppressed and of voiceless and marginalised people.'

At no point, however, does this document allow that birth control might help to control the explosion of Africa's population. This is not surprising: in the view of John Paul II, 'No personal or social circumstances have ever been able, or ever will be able, to rectify the moral wrong of the contraceptive act.'

Abortion has in his view remained entirely unacceptable. He told the Poles (and later repeated the judgement in Washington, where abortions apparently outnumber live births), 'If a person's right to life is violated at the moment in which he is first conceived in his mother's womb, an indirect blow is struck at the whole of the moral order, which serves to ensure the inviolable goods of man. Among those goods, life occupies the first place.' But the pope's view simply begged the question posed by others concerned with abortion of when a foetus becomes a person.

'Fundamentally, politics has an ethical dimension,' Pope John Paul II has consistently insisted. And, as he told some eighty thousand Catholics assembled in Yankee Stadium, New York, in October 1979, 'Social thinking and social practice inspired by the Gospel must always be marked by a special sensitivity towards those who are most in distress, those who are extremely poor, those suffering from all the physical, mental and moral ills that afflict humanity – including hunger, neglect, unemployment and despair.'

This stance led him to excoriate capitalism as well as communism. It even made him sensitive to some of the insights of supposedly disgraced Marxism. 'The supporters of capitalism in its extreme form,' he declared, 'tend to overlook the good things achieved by communism in its efforts to overcome unemployment and in its concern for the poor.' In 1981 John Paul II published an encyclical, *Laboram exercens*, calling for an economic order which would be neither capitalist nor Marxist but instead would be based on the dignity of labour and the rights of the workers.

So, it seemed, other traditions might find an echo in the views of the Holy Father. As he told the Ukrainians of Philadelphia, the various rites and traditions of the Church, its multiplicity of artistic expressions and liturgical insights, are not signs of disunity but reveal how the Holy Spirit continually enriches the lives of God's people. 'Catholic unity entails a recognition of the successor of St Peter and his ministry of strengthening and preserving intact the communion of the universal Church,' he said, 'while safeguarding the existence of legitimate individual traditions within it.' The pope added, 'It is precisely because these individual traditions are also intended for the enrichment of the universal Church that the apostolic see of Rome takes great care to protect and foster each one.'

This multiplicity might also include the insights of non-Catholic Churches. Even earlier, on 17 October 1978, the pope had told the conclave that elected him, 'We must not forget the brethren of other Churches and Christian confessions. The cause of ecumenicism is so lofty and such a sensitive issue that we may not remain silent about it. How often do we meditate together on the last wish of Christ, who asked the Father for the gift of unity for the disciples.' John Paul II pledged himself to try to remove whatever obstacles still remained in the way of Christian unity, so that, 'through common effort full communion may eventually be achieved.'

But doubts remain. Anglicans and Lutherans ordain women. In November 1955 the Vatican declared that the notion that women could be ordained did not belong to its 'store of faith'. Sixty-one per cent of American Catholics, polled in that year, favoured the ordination of women. The Vatican continued its opposition, even though a group of theologians convened by the pope in 1976 decided that nothing in holy scripture stood in the way of the ordination of women.

The pope still insisted on clerical celibacy, a rule introduced only in the eleventh century, a pattern of life contradicted by St Peter himself, who had taken a wife. This undoubtedly helps in part to explain the massive exodus of priests from the Church – some 100 thousand, it is estimated – under his reign. And this papal judgement made reconciliation between Catholicism and Protestantism seem yet more remote.

Yet in his encyclical *Ut unum sint*, John Paul II had invited the leaders of other Christian Churches to enter into dialogue with the Vatican to pave the way towards greater unity. Bartolomeus I, Orthodox Patriarch of Constantinople, responded by declaring that the papal office had become the greatest obstacle and threat to Christian unity. He was referring to the curia, which now seemed to regard itself as subordinate to the pope but superior to the rest of the Church. Since those whom a pope chooses to canonise or beatify also indicate his sympathies, it is apposite here to mention that in October 1996 John Paul II beatified sixteen Catholics, thirteen of whom were Poles who had been massacred by the troops of the Tsar for refusing to convert to Orthodoxy. These beatifications scarcely helped to endear John Paul II to the Orthodox.

If the ecumenical ambitions of the Holy Father came to naught, undoubtedly John Paul II was far more successful and influential in the break-up of the Soviet bloc and the collapse of communist autocracy in eastern Europe. Lech Walesa, the shipyard worker who defied the Bolsheviks in Poland and eventually became the country's president, derived consistent support from the pope and the Catholic Church, some of whose Polish priests would smuggle both instructions and provisions to the Gdansk strikers whom Walesa led.

John Paul II preserved a striking humility in his role in bringing down east European communism. 'The tree was already rotten,' he said. 'I just gave it a good shake.' Yet there is strong evidence that in the years before the break-up of Polish and east European communism the pope did meet emissaries of US President Ronald Reagan to collaborate in the demise of the eastern bloc.

The president himself visited John Paul II on 7 June 1972 and offered to collaborate with the Vatican in supporting Lech Walesa's Solidarity movement. But, say others, the pope declined the offer. Yet, as the former Soviet president, Mikhail Gorbachev said, everything that had happened in eastern Europe would have been impossible without the efforts of the pope and without the enormous role – including a political role – he had played on the world stage.

Yet the paradox remained of a pope passionately committed to freedom in the world who brooked not the slightest dissent in his own domain.

Glossary

Bull: the most solemn form of papal document on parchment and attached with silken cords to a leaden seal (*bulla*), on one side of which is depicted the reigning pontiff and on the other side Saints Peter and Paul.

Camerlengo: the official who administers the Church in a vacancy between two popes.

Collegiality: the belief that the whole episcopate bears corporate responsibility for the Church.

Conclave: a meeting of cardinals to elect a new pope.

Curia: the commissions and secretariats which assist the pope in his government of the Church.

Encyclical: a letter addressed to the pope's brother bishops or to all the faithful. John XXIII and Paul VI began the practice of addressing them to 'all those of good will'.

Exequatur: the rights over the life of the Church claimed in the past by civil authorities in their own territories.

Inter-confessionalism: thought and action linking Churches that have different confessions of faith.

Nuncio: a papal diplomat, usually a titular archbishop, representing the pope before both a civil government and the local Church.

Papabili: a description of those cardinals thought likely or eligible to be elected pope.

MAJOR ENCYCLICALS REFERRED TO IN THIS BOOK

Ad Anglos: to the English (1901)

Ad beatissimi: on the outbreak of the European War and on Modernism (1914)

Aeterni Patris: the philosophy of St Thomas Aquinas (1879)

Apostolicae curae: Anglican orders (1896)

Casti connubii: Christian marriage (1930)

Divini illius magistri: Christian education (1929)

Divini Redemptoris: atheistic communism (1937)

Divino afflante Spiritu: the promotion of Biblical studies (1943)

Firmissima constantiam: Mexico (1937)

Humani generis: false opinions (1959)

Humanae vitae: on the procreation of children (1968)

Laboram exercens: a just economic order (1981)

Lamentabilis sane exitu: the condemnation of Modernist errors (1907)

Mater et magistra: Christianity and social progress (1961)

Mystici corporis Christi: on the mystical body of Christ (1943)

Mit brennender Sorge: the Catholic Church in the Third Reich (1937)

Pacem Dei munus: on peace (1920)

Pacem in terris: peace on earth (1963)

Pascendi Dominici Gregis: on Modernism (1907)

Pieni l'animo: the clergy in Italy (1906)

Populorum Progressio: proper use of wealth (1964)
Princeps pastorum: missions (1959)
Providentissimus Deus: on the literal truth of the Bible (1893)
Quadrogesimo anno: the social order (1931)
Quas Primas: the feast of Christ the King (1925)
Rerum novarum: the condition of the working classes (1891)
Rerum Orientalium: reunion with the Eastern Orthodox Churches (1928)
Sacerdotalis coelibatus: clerical celibacy (1967)
Ut unum sint: Christian reunion (1981)

Bibliography

Dieter Albrecht (ed.), *Katholische Kirche im Dritten Reich*, 1976.

Robin Anderson, *Between Two Wars: The Story of Pope Pius XI*, 1977.

Anonymous, *The Persecution of the Catholic Church in the Third Reich*, 1940.

Carl Bernstein and Marco Politi, *His Holiness: John Paul II and the Hidden History of Our Time*, 1996.

Karl Heinz Deschner, *Die Vertreter Gottes: Eine Geschichte der Päpste im 20. Jahrhundert*, 1994.

Joseph F. Dinneen, *Pius XII: Pope of Peace*, 1939.

Carlo Falconi, *The Popes in the Twentieth Century: From Pius X to John XXIII*, 1967.

Carlo Falconi, *The Silence of Pius XII*, 1970.

F. A. Forbes, *Pope St Pius X*, fourth revised edition, 1954.

J. L. Gonzales, *A Portrait of Pope Montini*, 1966.

Jean Guitton, *The Pope Speaks*, 1968.

E. E. Y. Hales, *Pope John and his Revolution*, 1965.

Alden Hatch, *His name was John: A life of Pope John XXIII*, 1963.

Alden Hatch, *Pope Paul VI: Apostle on the Move*, 1967.

Peter Hebblethwaite, *Paul VI: The First Modern Pope*, 1993.

Peter Hebblethwaite and Ludwig Kaufmann, *John Paul II: A Pictorial Biography*, 1979.

Peter Hebblethwaite, *Pope John of the Council*, 1984.

Philip Hughes, *Pope Pius the Eleventh*, 1977.

John Paul II, *Pilgrimage of Peace: The Collected Speeches of John Paul II in Ireland and the United States*, 1980

Paul Johnson, *Pope John XXIII*, 1975.

Lord Longford, *Pope John Paul II: An Authorized Biography*, 1982.

Albino Luciani, *Illustrissimi: The Letters of Pope John Paul I*, translated by Isabel Quigly, 1978.

Leonard von Matt and Nello Vica, *St Pius X: A Pictorial Biography*, 1955.

Brian Murtogh (ed), *The Pope, the Pill, and the People*, 1968.

Michael O'Carroll, *Pius XII: Greatness Dishonoured*, 1980.

Carlo Napoli and Eugenio Marcucci, *Giovanni Paolo I: Papa per 33 Giorni*, 1978.

P. L. Occelli, *St Pius X*, 1956.

T. P. O'Mahoney, *The New Pope John Paul I: the Election, the Man & the Future*, 1978.

Walter H. Peters, *The Life of Benedict XV*, 1959.

The Polish Review, vol. XXIV, no. 2, New York, 1979: special issue dedicated to Karol Cardinal Wojtyla, John Paul II, Pontifex Maximus.

Anthony Rhodes, *The Vatican in the Age of the Dictators, 1922–45*, 1973.

Henry E. G. Ropes, *Benedict XV: The Pope of Peace*, 1940.

William Telling, *The Pope in Politics: The Life and Work of Pope Pius XI*, 1977.

Meriel Trevor, *Pope John*, 1967.
David Yallop, *In God's Name: An Investigation into the Murder of Pope John Paul I*, 1984.
Giancarlo Zizola, *Quale papa?* 1977.

Index